NEW
REMOSKA®
COOKING
FOR STANDARD AND GRAND REMOSKA

Published by
Hooray for Home Cooking Limited

First published in 2013

Hooray for Home Cooking Limited
PO Box 456
Preston Central
Preston
Lancashire
PR1 8GG

REMOSKA®

Remoska® is a registered trademark.

British Library Cataloguing in Publication Data.
A catalogue record for this book is available from the British Library.

ISBN No. 978-0-9544900-2-7

The moral rights of the authors have been asserted.

Editor
Milena Grenfell-Baines

Assistant Editor
Jill Wadeson

Recipes
Carol Wilson
Derek Smith

Design, artwork and art direction
Peter Gillett
Apartment Media and Print Limited

Photography
Paul Greenwood
Norwyn Limited

Food Styling
Rachael McNeela

Pre-press
NB Colour Print Limited

Printed in China through Asia Pacific Offset

Contents

Introduction 2

What is a Remoska? 3

General Tips 4

Wright's Baking Mixes 5

Conversion Tables 6

Energy Saving and Awards 7

Vegetables 9-27

Potatoes 29-41

Poultry and Game 43-59

Meat 61-79

Fish 81-91

Pasta and Rice 93-105

Cheese 107-113

Desserts 115-135

Baking 137-163

Index 165-169

Welcome to
NEW REMOSKA®
COOKING

If you have bought this book you will probably have the Remoska.

This clever small oven was invented in the 1950s in the Czech Republic and for years was its best kept secret. Today Czech people will tell you "Oh yes, my grandmother had one…"

For many years, when the country finally became free from the restrictive political system and western modern appliances were available to everyone, the Remoska was all but forgotten, until recent years when two engineers bought up the old machinery and began producing the Remoska once again.

Slowly people began to realise that this appliance cooks, roasts and bakes as well as any oven and uses much less energy. Not long after production began in the Czech Republic I introduced it to kitchenware company Lakeland and the Remoska came to the UK.

This new and updated version of the popular Remoska has had some recent cosmetic improvements and there is no longer a glass panel in the lid. Like an oven door it always required cleaning and, as the electric elements are in the lid, it cannot be immersed in water.

The new solid lid gives your cakes a more even colour (before the centre sometimes looked paler than the rim) and it cooks perfectly.

To ease yourself into using the Remoska start with something very simple, this will convince you how good this pan is, then enjoy trying out all the recipes in this book.

Lightly oil some jacket potatoes, place them in the Remoska, switch it on and sit down with a good book and a cup of tea. Soon (less than an hour, depending on size) you will have perfectly roasted jacket potatoes, golden crisp on the outside and fluffy soft on the inside, to have with any filling of your choice. Or put in two chicken legs on thick slices of potatoes and onions, there is your chicken dinner! Fish will poach in minutes and your scones will be perfect.

For much more information please visit our website at: **www.remoska.co.uk**

Milena Grenfell-Baines

Milena Grenfell-Baines

What is a Remoska?

The Remoska is an electric mini-oven with 'a lid that does the cooking'.

The lid houses the electric element, it sits on a Teflon® lined pan which has two handles and the pan rests on a flat stand.

There is a simple on/off switch on the handle; there is no graded heat control and yet it cooks just like (or even better than) a traditional oven and is amazingly economical with your energy consumption.

In addition to the Remoska, you may also purchase useful accessories such as a rack and extra deep or shallow pans.

The recipes are both for the **Standard** and the **Grand Remoska**.

The Remoska is NOT a slow cooker. Most foods will cook faster than in a normal oven. The timing of the recipes is approximate.

Sometimes the Remoska can be too efficient and with some recipes the cooking time needs extending. To slow down the cooking a foil plate placed over the contents will do the trick.

Onions and garlic fry well, it takes a little longer than a frying pan, but the onions will take on a lovely golden colour, just an occasional stir is necessary.

For quickly browning meat a frying pan is recommended.

Cakes may be baked directly in the tin or use a loose-based baking tin which will fit into the Remoska.

Cooking times are as a guide only. Times may vary depending on how thick your meat is or how finely chopped your other ingredients are.

General Tips

All food is cooked from cold unless otherwise stated.

You can roast any root vegetables, even cauliflower this way.

Ready-meals in oven-proof and foil containers, frozen food, especially pizzas and toasted sandwiches can be made in the Remoska.

Puff pastry and short crust pastry and pies generally are excellent in the Remoska.

Individual portions of food may be wrapped in lightly greased foil to cook separately.

Use the Remoska as a 'Bain Marie'.

If you need to take the lid off to stir, place it upside down away from you, using the fitted rest on the lid, it will be hot, like an oven door!

Do not heat the empty Remoska as with all Teflon® lined cooking pans, excess heating of an empty pan will damage the lining.

Never immerse the lid in water.

Wright's Baking Mixes

We are happy to announce we use Wright's Bread and Cake mixes in the Remoska, some recipes in this book have also used their products. Examples are Rosemary Focaccia on p158 and Sun Dried Tomato Rolls on p160.

Simply follow the instructions on the packet and use the Remoska instead of a traditional oven. A wide range is available from all major supermarkets.

Available in 500g and 1.5kg bags, see the Wright's website for more details:
www.wrightsflour.co.uk

Top Tip

When using the Remoska for baking, if you see the edges cooking/browning faster than the middle, use a ring of foil around the edges so the centre cooks a bit faster than the edges.

Conversion Tables

SOLID		LIQUID	
25g	1oz	25ml	1fl.oz
50g	2oz	50ml	2fl.oz
75g	3oz	75ml	3fl.oz
110g	4oz	100ml	4fl.oz
125g	4.5oz	125ml	4.5fl.oz
150g	5oz	150ml	5fl.oz
175g	6oz	175ml	6fl.oz
225g	8oz	200ml	7fl.oz
250g	9oz	225ml	8fl.oz
325g	12oz	250ml	8.5fl.oz
350g	12.5oz	275ml	½ pint
375g	13oz	300ml	10.5fl.oz
400g	14oz	350ml	12fl.oz
450g	1lb	400ml	14fl.oz
700g	1.5lbs	450ml	16fl.oz
1.1kg	2.5lbs	575ml	1pt

WEIGHT
AND VOLUME
EQUIVALENTS

VOLUME CONVERSIONS
Normally used for liquids only

1 teaspoon	5ml
1 tablespoon or ½ fluid ounce	15ml
1 fluid ounce or ⅛ cup	30ml
¼ cup or 2 fluid ounces	60ml
⅓ cup	80ml
½ cup or 4 fluid ounces	120ml
⅔ cup	160ml
¾ cup or 6 fluid ounces	180ml
1 cup or 8 fluid ounces or half a pint	240ml
1½ cups or 12 fluid ounces	250ml
2 cups or 1 pint or 16 fluid ounces	475ml
3 cups or 1½ pints	700ml
4 cups or 2 pints or 1 quart	950ml

Note: In cases where higher precision is not justified, it may be convenient to round these conversions off as follows:

1 cup = 250 ml   1 pint = 500 ml

Energy Saving

The New Remoska has undergone rigorous testing for its energy use and a recent report shows that electric ovens with energy consumption category A use 2,800 Watts.

The New Standard Remoska uses 400 Watts, a saving of 2,400W (85.7%).

The New Grand Remoska uses 580 Watts, a saving of 2,220W (79.3%).

A simple analogy to illustrate the energy saving aspect of the Remoska is to consider where a standard oven will use the power of 25 lightbulbs (100W) in normal use, the Remoska uses the power of **only 4 or 5 lightbulbs!**

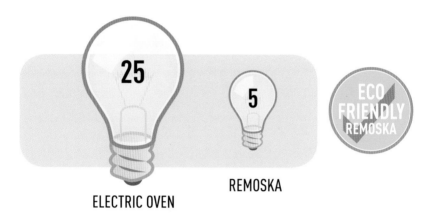

25

5

ECO FRIENDLY REMOSKA

REMOSKA

ELECTRIC OVEN

Awards

AWARD WINNING REMOSKA

The Remoska was one of the winners of the Good Housekeeping Innovations of the Year Award in 2001. Good Housekeeping wanted to encourage manufacturers to think more about how products are used in real life, and readers were asked to submit genuinely innovative new products that had improved their lives.

GHI testers were impressed, rating it very highly and declaring that a Victoria sponge cake, fried chicken and poached salmon all worked well in the Remoska, a useful back-up and a great idea for caravan holidays. Versatile and compact, cooking results are as good as with a normal oven.

Vegetables

Baked Polenta with Spinach and Cheese

Ingredients	Standard	Grand
Tomato passata	350g	500g
Frozen spinach, thawed	300g	450g
Salt and pepper		
Ready-made polenta, sliced	500g	750g
Olive oil	1tbsp	2tbsp
Mozzarella cheese, grated	100g	200g

Method

Put the passata into the Remoska.

Season the spinach with salt and pepper and spoon on top of the passata.

Arrange the polenta slices on top and drizzle with the oil. Cook for **20 minutes,** then sprinkle with the cheese and cook for a **further 10 minutes,** until the cheese is golden and bubbling.

spinach

Baked Sweet Potatoes and Apples

Ingredients	Standard	Grand
Sweet potatoes, peeled	675g	1kg
Salt	$\frac{1}{2}$tsp	$\frac{3}{4}$tsp
Eating apples	4	6
Salt and pepper		
Lemon juice	1tbsp	$1\frac{1}{2}$tbsp
Butter	50g	75g
Cider	125ml	185ml

Method

Cut the sweet potatoes into 1.5cm slices and place in a pan of boiling water with the salt. Cook for **5 minutes**, then drain.

Cut the apples into small dice and toss in the lemon juice.

Arrange half the sweet potatoes in the base of the Remoska and cover with a layer of apples, then add the remaining potatoes. Season the layers to taste with salt and pepper.

Heat together the butter and cider until the butter has melted. Pour the mixture over the potatoes and cook for **approx 30-40 minutes** until tender.

Braised Little Gem Lettuce

Ingredients	Standard	Grand
Little Gem lettuce	6	10
Salt and pepper		
Vegetable stock	200ml	300ml
Olive oil	4tbsp	6tbsp
Rosemary sprigs	3	5

Method

Put the whole lettuces into the Remoska and season with salt and pepper.

Pour in the stock and drizzle with the oil.

Add the rosemary sprigs. Cook for **approx 15-20 minutes**, until the lettuce is wilted and tender.

rosemary

Broccoli and Cauliflower Soufflés

Ingredients	Standard	Grand
Cheddar cheese, grated	110g	175g
Cauliflower florets	110g	175g
Broccoli florets	110g	175g
Salt and pepper		
Milk	100ml	150ml
Cream cheese with herbs and garlic	55g	75g
Butter	40g	60g
Flour, plain	40g	60g
Mustard, Dijon	1tbsp	1½tbsp
Eggs, large, separated	3	4

Method

Cook the cauliflower and broccoli in boiling salted water for **approx 7-8 minutes** until just tender. Drain, refresh under cold running water and drain well. Mash the vegetables with the milk and cream cheese to a purée, or blend in a food processor.

Melt the butter in a pan, stir in the flour and cook for **30 seconds.** Remove from the heat, stir in the vegetable purée and season with salt and pepper. Return to the heat and bring to the boil, stirring continuously until thickened. Stir in the mustard and set aside to cool slightly.

Stir in the egg yolks, one at a time until blended. Stir in the grated cheese until combined.

Whisk the egg whites until stiff, and gently fold into the sauce. Spoon into 4 buttered deep ramekins and place in the Remoska. Pour in enough hot water to reach halfway up the sides of the dishes. Cook for **approx 25-30 minutes**, until risen and puffy.

Serve immediately.

Broccoli and Cheese Calzone

Ingredients	Standard and Grand
Flour, strong, plain	250g
Salt	1tsp
Yeast, easy-blend	1tsp
Water, warm	175ml
Olive oil	1tbsp
Egg, beaten	1
Broccoli spears	300g
Parmesan cheese, grated	175g
Salt and pepper	

Method

Mix together the flour, salt and yeast. Add the water and oil and mix to a soft dough.

Turn out and knead for **approx 10 minutes,** until the dough is smooth and elastic. Put into a greased bowl, cover and leave in a warm place for **approx 40 minutes** until doubled in size.

Turn out and knead the dough for **approx 2-3 minutes.**

Blanch the broccoli in boiling salted water for **2 minutes.** Drain and rinse under cold running water, then drain well. Roughly chop the broccoli.

Divide the dough in half. Roll out each half on a floured surface to a 23cm round. Brush each round with a little olive oil.

Divide the broccoli between each round of dough, keeping it on one half of each round. Sprinkle the rounds with cheese and season with salt and pepper.

Brush the edges of the dough with beaten egg and fold over to form semi-circles. Press well to seal the edges. Brush with the remaining beaten egg and cut a slit in the top of each.

Put into the Remoska (1 at a time in the Standard and 2 in the Grand). Cook for **approx 30-35 minutes** until golden brown and cooked through.

Caponata

Ingredients	Standard	Grand
Olive oil	3tbsp	4tbsp
Aubergine, cubed	2	3
Onions, chopped	2	3
Celery sticks, chopped	2	3
Olives, pitted	2-3tbsp	3-4tbsp
Tomatoes, chopped	4	6
Salt and pepper		
Sugar	1tbsp	1½tbsp
Red wine vinegar	3tbsp	4½tbsp
Caper berries, rinsed	1tbsp	1½tbsp

Method

Heat the oil in the Remoska and add the aubergines.

Cook for **15 minutes**, then add the onions and celery and cook for **another 10 minutes**. Add the olives, tomatoes, salt and pepper and cook for **15 minutes**.

Add the sugar, vinegar and caper berries, stir well and cook for **approx 10-15 minutes** until the vegetables are soft.

Serve at room temperature, drizzled with olive oil.

Chicory with Pears

Ingredients	Standard	Grand
Chicory	4	6
Pears	2	3
Lemon juice	1tbsp	2tbsp
Butter	40g	60g
Olive oil	1½tbsp	2tbsp
Sugar	2tsp	3tsp

Method

Put the chicory in the Remoska. Peel and core the pears and cut into halves or quarters (if large). Put into the Remoska.

Sprinkle with lemon juice and dot the butter over the chicory. Drizzle with the oil and sprinkle with sugar.

Cook in the Remoska for **20 minutes**, then turn the chicory and pears over and cook for a **further 15-20 minutes** until the chicory is tender.

Chorizo and Couscous Stuffed Squash

Ingredients	Grand
Butternut squash	1
Olive oil	2tbsp
Onion, finely chopped	1
Chorizo, diced	100g
Couscous	100g
Lemon, juice only	1
Water, boiling	
Pepper, roasted red, drained and sliced	2
Mint, chopped	1tbsp
Coriander, chopped	1tbsp
Salt and pepper	

Method

Cut the squash in half through the middle and scoop out the seeds.

Cut out some of the flesh, to about one third of the way down and dice the flesh.

Heat the oil in the Remoska and add the onion and diced squash. Cook for **approx 10-15 minutes** until softened. Add the chorizo and cook for a **further 5 minutes.**

Meanwhile, put the couscous in a bowl and stir in the lemon juice. Pour in enough boiling water to just cover. Stir, cover with clingfilm and leave to stand for **5 minutes** until the liquid has been absorbed.

Add the onion mixture to the couscous with the diced red pepper and herbs. Season to taste with salt and pepper.

Put the squash halves into the Remoska. Spoon the couscous into the hollows and on the flesh to cover, pressing down with a spoon.

Cook for **approx 40-50 minutes** until the squash is tender.

Honey, Lemon and Thyme Roasted Root Vegetables

Ingredients	Standard	Grand
Carrots	400g	600g
Parsnips	200g	300g
Swede	200g	300g
Salt and pepper		
Lemon juice	3tbsp	4tbsp
Olive oil	4tbsp	6tbsp
Thyme	2tbsp	3tbsp
Thyme honey	3tbsp	4tbsp
Vegetable stock	50ml	75ml

Method

Halve or quarter the vegetables lengthwise, depending on size.

Mix with the salt, pepper, lemon juice, olive oil, thyme and honey.

Put into the Remoska, pour over the stock and cook for **approx 1-1$\frac{1}{4}$ hours**, turning occasionally until most of the stock is absorbed and the vegetables are tender.

honey

Lamb Stuffed Peppers in Cheese Sauce

Ingredients	Standard	Grand
Peppers	2	3
Onion, finely chopped	1	1½
Lamb, minced	400g	600g
Breadcrumbs, fresh	2tbsp	3tbsp
Salt and pepper		
Worcestershire sauce	1tsp	2tsp
Rosemary, finely chopped	1tsp	2tsp
Olive oil	1tbsp	1½tbsp
Cheese sauce, tub	250g	375g

Method

Cut the peppers in half lengthways and remove the seeds. Mix together the onion, lamb, breadcrumbs, salt and pepper to taste, Worcestershire sauce and rosemary.

Spoon into the pepper halves, pressing down lightly.

Drizzle the oil into the Remoska and add the peppers. Cook for **approx 35-40 minutes** until the peppers are just tender. Add the cheese sauce, spooning it around the peppers and cook for a **further 15 minutes** until the sauce is bubbling.

Leeks Wrapped in Smoked Bacon

Ingredients	Standard	Grand
Leeks	4	8
Bacon, smoked, thinly sliced rashers	4	8
Cheese, Cheddar	100g	200g
Mustard, Dijon	1tbsp	2tbsp
Crème fraiche	4tbsp	7tbsp

Method

Cook the leeks in a pan of boiling water for no more than **5 minutes.**

Drain and cool under a cold tap, drain again and pat dry on kitchen paper.

Wrap a strip of the smoked bacon around each leek and arrange in the Remoska. Mix the cheddar in a bowl with the mustard and the crème fraiche until well combined. Season to taste.

Cook the leeks for **10 minutes** and then drizzle a little cheese sauce over the leeks and around them and cook for a **further 15-20 minutes.**

Serve at once.

Peppers Stuffed with Chicken, Bacon and Rice

Ingredients	Standard	Grand
Peppers	2	4
Oil	2tbsp	3tbsp
Onion, chopped	1	1½
Chicken breasts, diced	2	4
Pancetta cubetti	35g	70g
Rice, cooked	75g	110g
Stock, chicken	100ml	150ml
Salt and pepper		
Cheese, Cheddar, grated	75g	175g

Method

Cut the peppers in half; remove the seeds and membranes.

Heat 1tbsp of oil in a frying pan and cook the onion until softened but not browned. Remove the onion from the pan.

Add the chicken and pancetta to the pan and cook until browned.

Brush the outsides of the pepper halves with a little oil.

Mix the onion, chicken, pancetta and rice with the stock and season to taste with salt and pepper. Spoon into the pepper halves. Sprinkle with grated cheese and drizzle with the remaining oil.

Put into the Remoska and cook for **approx 40-45 minutes** until the peppers are tender and the cheese is bubbling.

peppers

Roast Baby Cabbages with Honey and Balsamic Vinegar

Ingredients	Standard	Grand
Cabbage, baby	2	4
Salt and pepper		
Balsamic vinegar	2tbsp	4tbsp
Honey	2tbsp	3-4tbsp
Butter	100g	175g

Method

Cut the cabbages in half, season with salt and pepper and place in the Remoska.

Put the balsamic vinegar, honey and butter in a pan and warm gently until the butter and honey have melted. Stir and pour over the cabbage halves.

Cook in the Remoska for **20 minutes.** Turn the cabbages over and cook for a **further 15-20 minutes** (depending on size) until the cabbage is tender.

Souffléd Tomatoes

Ingredients	Standard	Grand
Tomatoes, beef	6	9
Butter	40g	60g
Flour, plain	30g	45g
Milk	200ml	300ml
Salt and pepper (white)		
Mustard powder	$\frac{1}{4}$tsp	$\frac{1}{2}$tsp
Eggs, separated	3	4
Cheese, Red Leicester	55g	75g
Cheese, Parmesan, grated	1tbsp	2tbsp

Method

Slice the tops off the tomatoes and scoop out the core, flesh and seeds.

Stand the tomato shells upside down on absorbent kitchen paper to drain.

Melt the butter in a pan and stir in the flour. Cook gently for **1 minute**, then whisk in the milk. Bring to the boil, whisking constantly and simmer for **2 minutes**. Remove from the heat and allow to cool slightly.

Beat in the salt, pepper, mustard powder, egg yolks and Red Leicester cheese until well blended and the cheese has melted.

Whisk the egg whites until stiff and gradually fold into the warm cheese mixture.

Spoon the mixture into the tomato shells and sprinkle with the Parmesan cheese.

Place in the Remoska and cook for **approx 20 minutes** until the filling is puffy and golden. Serve immediately.

Spicy Sweet Potato Wedges

Ingredients	Standard	Grand
Cumin	1tsp	2tsp
Coriander	1tsp	2tsp
Cinnamon	$\frac{1}{2}$tsp	1tsp
Allspice	1tsp	2tsp
Sugar	1tsp	2tsp
Salt	$\frac{1}{2}$tsp	1tsp
Black pepper	$\frac{1}{2}$tsp	1tsp
Oil	2tbsp	3tbsp
Sweet potatoes, large, peeled and cut into wedges	2	4

Method

Put the spices, salt and pepper in a large plastic food bag and shake well.

Add the potato wedges and shake well until evenly coated.

Put half the oil into the Remoska and add the wedges. Sprinkle with the remaining oil.

Cook for **approx 30-35 minutes,** turning halfway during cooking, until the wedges are tender.

coriander

Stuffed Aubergines

Ingredients	Standard	Grand
Aubergines	2	4
Pancetta, diced	90g	150g
Mozzarella cheese, sliced	125g	250g
Onion, thinly sliced	1	1
Oil		

Method

Cut slits in the aubergines but don't cut through the base.

Place the pancetta, cheese slices and onion slices in the slits and put into the Remoska.

Drizzle with a little oil and cook for **approx 40 minutes** until the aubergines are tender and the filling is bubbling.

Stuffed Pancakes

Ingredients	Standard	Grand
Olive oil	1tbsp	2tbsp
Garlic cloves, finely chopped	2	4
Spinach, frozen, thawed, chopped	100g	300g
Salt		
Black pepper		
Nutmeg, freshly grated		
Pancakes	4	6
Garlic and herb soft cheese	125g	250g
Tomato passata	300g	600g
Cheese, Parmesan, grated	2tbsp	4tbsp

Method

Heat the oil in the Remoska and cook the garlic until softened. Squeeze the excess liquid from the spinach and put into a bowl. Season with salt, pepper and nutmeg.

Spread the garlic and herb cheese on the pancakes and top with the spinach. Roll up into tubes. Spoon half the passata into the Remoska and stir into the garlic.

Place the pancakes on top, add the remaining passata and sprinkle with Parmesan cheese.

Cook in the Remoska for **approx 25 minutes**, until the sauce and filling is piping hot and bubbling.

Summer Vegetable Gratin

Ingredients	Standard	Grand
Courgettes, cut into small chunks	2	3
Baby carrots	8-10	12-15
Cherry tomatoes	8	12
Shallots, halved if large	6	9
Salt and pepper		
Pesto	5tbsp	7tbsp
Mustard, Dijon	1tbsp	$1\frac{1}{2}$tbsp

Method

Put the vegetables into the Remoska and season with salt and pepper. Add the pesto and mustard and stir well to coat the vegetables.

Cook for **approx 45 minutes**, until the vegetables are tender.

Serve hot or warm.

Vegetable Frittata

Ingredients	Standard	Grand
Olive oil	1tbsp	1½tbsp
Potato, large diced	1	2
Pepper, chopped	1	2
Onion, chopped	1	2
Celery sticks, diced	2	3
Garlic, chopped	1	2
Cream, double	200ml	300ml
Eggs, beaten	5	7
Cheese, Parmesan, grated	55g	80g
Salt and pepper		

Method

Heat the oil in the Remoska and cook the potatoes, pepper, onions, celery and garlic for **approx 10-15 minutes** until softened.

Beat together the cream and eggs and stir in the cheese. Season to taste with salt and pepper.

Pour over the vegetables and bake for **approx 15 minutes** until golden on top and the eggs have set.

Wine Braised Fennel with Parmesan and Walnuts

Ingredients	Standard	Grand
Butter	50g	100g
Fennel bulbs, halved	2	4
Salt and pepper		
Wine, dry white	5tbsp	10tbsp
Cheese, Parmesan, grated	4tbsp	8tbsp
Cheese, Gruyère, grated	2tbsp	4tbsp
Walnuts, chopped	2-3tbsp	4-6tbsp

Method

Melt the butter in the Remoska. Season the fennel with salt and pepper and place in the Remoska. Pour over the wine.

Cook for **approx 30 minutes**, turning halfway through cooking, until the fennel is tender.

Sprinkle with the cheese and walnuts and cook for a **further 10 minutes** until the cheese has melted and the walnuts are toasted.

parmesan

Potatoes

Classic Pommes Anna
Simple French Gratin Potato Cake

Ingredients	Standard
Potatoes, Maris Piper (or similar), peeled and very thinly sliced	1kg
Butter, melted	225g
Salt	
Black pepper, freshly ground	

Method

Put the potato slices in a colander and rinse under running water to get rid of the starch. Place on a cloth in a single layer and pat dry.

Generously grease the base of the Remoska with melted butter.

Arrange the potato slices in the Remoska in overlapping circles, brushing butter over each layer and seasoning as you go. Alternate the overlapping slices on each layer.

Cover with greaseproof paper or a lid. Cook for **approx 45-60 minutes** until the potatoes are cooked, testing with a skewer.

Creamy Cheese Potato Bake

Ingredients	Grand
Potatoes	1½kg
Onion, finely chopped	1
Butter	25g
Wine, white	100ml
Milk	250ml
Cream, double	400ml
Salt and pepper	
Sage leaves, torn	3
Cheese, Gruyère, grated	55g

Method

Cook the potatoes in a pan of boiling water for **3 minutes**. Peel when cool enough to handle and slice thinly.

Put the butter into the Remoska and cook the onion for **approx 10 minutes** until softened. Pour in the wine, milk, cream and sage, season with salt and pepper and stir well. Stir in the potatoes, stirring gently until the slices are coated in the cream mixture.

Cook in the Remoska for **45 minutes**. Sprinkle over the cheese and cook for a **further 20-25 minutes** until the potatoes are tender.

Switch off the Remoska and leave to stand for **10 minutes** before serving.

milk

Fluffy Potato Pancakes

Ingredients	Standard or Grand
Floury potatoes, peeled, cut into chunks	200g
Salt and pepper	
Milk	100ml
Flour, plain	2tbsp
Eggs	2
Egg whites	1
Cream, double	4tbsp
Vegetable oil	

Method

Cook the potatoes in a pan of boiling salted water until tender.

Drain well.

Mash the potatoes, season with salt and pepper and beat in the milk. Whisk in the flour and eggs, one at a time until smooth, then whisk in the egg white. Beat in the cream, then cover and leave to stand for **20 minutes.**

Heat a thin layer of oil in the Remoska. Pour in a layer of batter, about 5mm thick. Cook for **a few minutes** until set.

Cut out rounds with a 6cm cutter and continue cooking for **approx 10-15 minutes** on each side until browned and cooked through.

Repeat with the remaining batter. Alternatively, you can make large pancakes, turning halfway through.

Indian Spiced Potatoes

Ingredients	Standard	Grand
Waxy potatoes, peeled, cut into chunks	600g	900g
Vegetable oil	1tbsp	$1\frac{1}{2}$tbsp
Butter	2tbsp	3tbsp
Cardamom pods, cracked	8	12
Mustard seeds	1tsp	$1\frac{1}{2}$tsp
Coriander seeds	1tsp	$1\frac{1}{4}$tsp
Turmeric	1tsp	$1\frac{1}{2}$tsp
Garam masala	$\frac{1}{2}$tsp	1tsp
Onion salt	$\frac{1}{2}$tsp	1tsp
Salt and pepper		

Method

Parboil the potatoes in a pan of boiling salted water for **4 minutes.**

Drain well.

Heat the butter and oil in the Remoska. Add the spices and onion salt and stir well.

Add the potatoes and stir until coated.

Cook for **approx 30-35 minutes** until the potatoes are tender and golden.

Season with salt and pepper.

cardamom

Latkes

Ingredients	Standard	Grand
Potatoes, large, cut into chunks	3	5
Onion, large, chopped	1	$1\frac{1}{2}$
Eggs	2	3
Salt	1tsp	$1\frac{1}{2}$tsp
Pepper	$\frac{1}{2}$tsp	1tsp
Flour, plain	3tbsp	$4\frac{1}{2}$tbsp
Vegetable oil		

Method

Put the potatoes and onion into a food processor and blend until finely chopped but not 'gluey'. Add the eggs, salt and pepper and flour and process until blended.

Heat a thin layer of oil in the Remoska. Drop spoonfuls of the mixture, apart, into the Remoska and cook for **approx 15 minutes** until golden on the underside. Turn over and cook for **approx 10 minutes** until golden and crisp.

Drain on absorbent kitchen paper.

Repeat until all the mixture is used.

Lemon and Thyme Potatoes

Ingredients	Standard	Grand
Potatoes, large, sliced	4	6
Lemons, zest and juice	2	3
Olive oil	2tbsp	3tbsp
Butter, melted	25g	40g
Thyme, chopped	2tbsp	3tbsp
Garlic cloves, crushed	2	3
Salt and pepper		

Method

Put the potatoes into the Remoska and scatter with the lemon zest.

Pour over the lemon juice, oil and butter and sprinkle with the thyme and garlic. Season to taste with salt and pepper.

Cook for **approx 40-45 minutes,** turning halfway through until the potatoes are tender and browned on top.

lemon

Mini Rostis

Ingredients	Standard	Grand
Baking potatoes, large	2	4
Butter, melted	3tbsp	6tbsp
Thyme, chopped	1tbsp	2tbsp
Garlic clove, crushed	1	2
Salt and pepper		

Method

Boil the potatoes in their skins for **6 minutes** and leave to cool.

This can be done the day before.

Peel the potatoes and grate into a bowl. Stir in 2 tablespoons of melted butter, the thyme and garlic. Season with salt and pepper.

Spoon into 6 lightly buttered silicone cupcake cases (12 for the Grand) and drizzle over the remaining butter.

Put into the Remoska and cook for **approx 30 minutes** until the potatoes are tender and browned on top.

Potato and Fennel Boulangère

Ingredients	Standard	Grand
Butter	50g	75g
Olive oil	1tbsp	1½tbsp
Fennel bulb, sliced	1	2
Onion, thinly sliced	1	2
Salt and pepper		
Waxy potatoes, thinly sliced	600g	900g
Stock, vegetable	500ml	700ml

Method

Melt the butter in the Remoska.

Season the fennel and onions with salt and pepper and place in the Remoska. Cook for **approx 20 minutes,** stirring halfway through cooking. Remove from the Remoska and place on a plate.

Add the oil to the Remoska and arrange a layer of potatoes over the base. Season with salt and pepper. Top with the fennel mixture.

Arrange the remaining potatoes over the top and season again. Pour over the stock and cook for **approx 45-50 minutes** until the vegetables are tender.

Potato and Red Wine Galette

Ingredients	Standard	Grand
Olive oil	2tbsp	3tbsp
Potatoes, waxy, peeled and sliced	500g	750g
Salt and pepper		
Garlic cloves, crushed	2	3
Thyme, chopped	½tbsp	1tbsp
Wine, red	300ml	450ml

Method

Put half the oil in the Remoska.

Arrange half the potato slices on the base and season with salt and pepper. Scatter with the garlic and thyme. Arrange the remaining potatoes on top, season to taste and pour in the wine.

Drizzle the remaining oil over the potatoes and cook for **approx 45-50 minutes** until the potatoes are tender.

Potato Daube

Ingredients	Standard	Grand
Garlic cloves, crushed	4	6
Water	200ml	300ml
Salt and pepper		
Olive oil	4tbsp	6tbsp
Potatoes, peeled, sliced	900g	1.3kg
Thyme sprigs	3	4

Method

Put the garlic cloves, water and salt into a pan and bring to the boil. Simmer gently for **15 minutes**. Press the garlic through a sieve back into the cooking water.

Put half the olive oil into the Remoska and add half the potatoes. Sprinkle with the thyme and a little salt and pepper.

Add the remaining potatoes and the sieved garlic and cooking water.

The potatoes should be covered.

Drizzle with the remaining oil and cook in the Remoska for **approx 50-60 minutes** until the potatoes are browned. If the potatoes become too dry during cooking (depending on the type of potatoes used) add a little more water.

garlic

Potato Gratin with Pancetta

Ingredients	Standard	Grand
Potatoes, peeled and thinly sliced	500g	750g
Salt and pepper		
Pancetta, diced	100g	150g
Garlic cloves, crushed	2	3
Cream, whipping	300ml	450ml
Cornflour	$\frac{1}{2}$tbsp	1tbsp
Butter	15g	20g
Cheese, Gruyère	75g	100g

Method

Cook the potatoes in a pan of boiling salted water for **2 minutes**. Drain well and put into the Remoska. Season with salt and pepper.

Cook the pancetta in a dry frying pan until browned and almost crisp. Drain well on kitchen paper.

Sprinkle the pancetta and garlic over the potatoes.

Whisk the cream with the cornflour until blended. Pour over the potatoes and dot with butter. Cook in the Remoska for **approx 20 minutes**.

Scatter over the cheese and cook for a **further 10-15 minutes** until the cheese is melted and the potatoes are tender.

Savoury Potato Cake

Ingredients	Standard	Grand
Pancetta	70g	100g
Onion, large, chopped	1	1½
Mushrooms	125g	185g
Thyme, chopped	2tbsp	3tbsp
Potatoes	750g	1kg
Butter, melted	75g	100g
Salt and pepper		

Method

Put the pancetta into a frying pan and heat gently until the fat runs. Add the onion and mushrooms and cook for **approx 5-10 minutes** until cooked. Remove from the heat and stir in the thyme. Leave to cool.

Peel the potatoes and slice very thinly (a food processor is best for this). Put into a bowl and mix in the melted butter. Season generously with salt and pepper.

Put half the potatoes in the Remoska. Spoon the pancetta mixture on top, leaving a 1cm border.

Put the remaining potatoes on top and press down. Cook in the Remoska for **approx 45-55 minutes,** until the potatoes are tender and the base is crisp and brown and the top is lightly browned. Switch off the Remoska and leave to cool slightly for a few minutes.

Serve from the Remoska or invert onto a large plate and cut into wedges.

Spiced Sweet Potatoes

Ingredients	Standard	Grand
Butter	55g	75g
Olive oil	1tbsp	1½tbsp
Sweet potatoes, peeled and diced	600g	900g
Cardamom pods, cracked	6	9
Mustard seeds	1tsp	1½tsp
Coriander seeds	1tsp	1½tsp
Cloves	3	5
Curry paste	1-2tsp	2-3tsp
Bay leaves	2	3
Salt and pepper		

Method

Heat the butter and oil in the Remoska. Toss the sweet potatoes with the spices and curry paste.

Put into the Remoska with the bay leaves and stir well.

Cook for **approx 30-35 minutes,** until the sweet potatoes are tender.

Season to taste with salt and pepper.

bay leaf

Poultry
& Game

Abruzzi Chicken

Ingredients	Standard	Grand
Chicken thighs	6	9
Black pepper		
Salt		
Olive oil	1tbsp	1½tbsp
Pancetta, diced	90g	135g
Rosemary	2 sprigs	3 sprigs
Sage	3 sprigs	4 sprigs
Bay leaves	3	4
Garlic cloves, chopped	3	4
Cloves	4	6
Wine, dry white	240ml	360ml

Method

Season the chicken with salt and pepper. In a frying pan brown the chicken on all sides in 1 tablespoon of oil. Transfer into the Remoska. Scatter over the remaining ingredients and pour in the wine.

Cook for **approx 30-40 minutes** until the chicken is tender and the liquid is reduced.

Remove the herb sprigs, bay leaves and cloves before serving.

garlic

Chicken and Tomato Bake with Basil

Ingredients	Standard	Grand
Chicken legs	2	4
Salt and pepper		
Basil	½ bunch	1 bunch
Red pepper, deseeded, sliced	1	2
Cherry tomatoes, halved	6	12
Olive oil		

Method

Season the chicken with salt and pepper and put into the Remoska.

Add the remaining ingredients, drizzling with the olive oil.

Cook in the Remoska for **approx 30-40 minutes** until the chicken is cooked through.

Chicken Breasts Stuffed
with Basil, Tomatoes and Boursin Cheese

Ingredients	Standard	Grand
Chicken breasts, skinless, boneless	4	6
Sun-dried tomatoes in oil,		
drained (reserve the oil)	75g	100g
Cheese, Boursin	100g	150g
Garlic cloves, finely chopped	2	3
Fresh basil, bunch torn		
Salt and pepper		

Method

Cut a deep slit with a sharp knife along the length of each chicken breast to form a pocket.

Fill each pocket with alternate layers of sun-dried tomatoes, cheese, garlic and basil, secure with a cocktail stick.

Season with salt and pepper and scatter with the remaining garlic and basil. Drizzle over 2tbsp of the oil from the tomatoes.

Put into the Remoska and cook for **approx 25-35 minutes,** until the chicken breasts are tender and the juices run clear when pierced.

basil

Chicken Curry

Ingredients	Standard	Grand
Chicken thighs, boneless, skinless	6	10
Oil	1tbsp	2tbsp
Butter	25g	40g
Onions, finely chopped	2	3
Garlic, cloves crushed	4	6
Chilli, red, sliced, deseeded	1	1-2
Cumin	1tsp	$1\frac{1}{2}$tsp
Cardamom seeds, crushed	3tsp	5tsp
Turmeric, ground	2tsp	3tsp
Garam masala	2tsp	3tsp
Ginger, fresh, grated	1tsp	2tsp
Flour	1tbsp	2tbsp
Salt	1tsp	$1\frac{1}{2}$tsp
Bay leaves, crushed	2	3
Stock, chicken	200ml	300ml
Chickpeas, tin (425g)	1	2

To garnish:
Coriander leaves

Method

Cut each thigh into 4 pieces. Heat the oil in a frying pan and brown the chicken pieces. Remove from the pan and put into the Remoska.

Add the butter to the pan and when hot add the onions, garlic and chilli. Cook until just beginning to colour, then add the spices, flour and salt. Cook for **1 minute.** Add the bay leaves and stock. Stir in the chickpeas.

Pour the mixture into the Remoska to cover the chicken.

Cook for **approx 35-45 minutes** until the chicken is tender.

Chicken Galantine

Ingredients	Standard	Grand
Back bacon rashers	8-10	16-20
Sausage meat	500g	1kg
Chicken breasts, boneless, skinless	2	4
Salt and pepper	1tbsp	2tbsp
Thyme, chopped		

Method

Lay the bacon rashers down the centre of a large sheet of non-stick baking paper.

Pat half the sausage meat in an even layer down the centre of the bacon. Flatten the chicken breasts with a rolling pin and lay on top of the sausage meat. Season with salt and pepper and sprinkle with thyme. Pat the remaining sausage meat on top of the chicken. Wrap over the bacon rashers.

Shape into a roll in the non-stick baking paper and seal the edges tightly. Cook in the Remoska for **30 minutes**.

Open the paper and cook for **another 35-40 minutes** until the meat is cooked and the bacon is browned.

Switch off the Remoska and leave the galantine to cool in the Remoska.

Serve cold, cut into slices.

(For the Grand: make 2 separate rolls and cook as above).

Chicken with Mushrooms

Ingredients	Standard	Grand
Flour, plain	2tsp	3tsp
Mushrooms, Porcini, dried	35g	50g
Stock, chicken, hot	200ml	300ml
Onion, cut into wedges	1	2
Garlic cloves, chopped	2	3
Thyme, chopped	1tbsp	$1\frac{1}{2}$tbsp
Mushrooms, mixed, quartered	400g	600g
Chicken fillets	500g	750g
Butter, diced	25g	40g
Wine, dry white	60ml	90ml
Salt	$\frac{1}{2}$tsp	$\frac{3}{4}$tsp
Freshly ground black pepper	1tsp	$1\frac{1}{2}$tsp

Method

Put the flour into a roasting bag and shake gently to coat. Add the dried mushrooms and pour in the hot chicken stock. Add the onion, garlic and thyme and shake the bag gently. Add the mixed mushrooms, chicken, butter, wine, salt and pepper.

Seal the top of the bag with the heat-proof ties supplied. Leave a tiny air gap or the bag may burst while cooking.

Put into the Remoska and cook for **approx 30-35 minutes** until the mushrooms are tender and the chicken is cooked.

mushrooms

Lemon Thyme Poussin

Ingredients	Standard	Grand
Poussin	2	4
Butter	50g	100g
Thyme sprigs	10	15
Salt and pepper		
Potatoes, large, sliced	3-4	4-5
Stock, chicken	50-75ml	75-100ml

Method

Rub the poussin all over with the butter. Put 3 thyme sprigs into each bird and a wedge of lemon. Season to taste with salt and pepper. Arrange the potatoes in the base of the Remoska and sprinkle with salt and pepper. Sprinkle with the remaining thyme.

Place the poussin on top of the potatoes. Squeeze the remaining lemon wedges over the poussin and potatoes.

Pour in the stock. Cook in the Remoska for **approx 1 hour,** until the poussin are cooked and the potatoes are tender and most of the stock has been absorbed. If the potatoes look a little dry during cooking, add more stock.

Minted Yoghurt Chicken

Ingredients	Standard	Grand
Mint, chopped	3tbsp	4tbsp
Chives, snipped	3tbsp	5tbsp
Yoghurt, plain	150ml	225ml
Oil	2tbsp	3tbsp
Garlic clove, crushed	1	2
Salt and black pepper		
Chicken breasts, boneless	2	3-4
Apricots, dried, chopped, (no need to soak)	110g	175g

Method

Mix together the mint, chives, yoghurt, oil, garlic and salt and pepper to taste. Turn the chicken breasts in the mixture until coated. Cover and leave for at least **4 hours** or overnight, turning occasionally.

Remove the chicken from the marinade (reserve the rest of the marinade) and put into the Remoska. Cook for **approx 20 minutes.**

Stir the apricots into the remaining marinade and spoon over the chicken. Cook for a **further 15-20 minutes,** until the chicken is cooked through and there are no pink juices.

Pancetta Wrapped Chicken with Leeks

Ingredients	Standard	Grand
Butter	25g	50g
Oil	½tbsp	1tbsp
Leeks, sliced	4	6-8
Thyme sprigs		
Wine, white	2tbsp	4tbsp
Chicken breast, skinless, boneless	2	4
Salt and pepper		
Pancetta slices	6	12

Method

Heat the butter and oil in the Remoska and when melted add the leeks and thyme sprigs. Cook in the Remoska for **15 minutes** until softened. Stir in the wine.

Season the chicken with salt and pepper.

Lay 3 pancetta slices on a work surface and place a chicken breast on top. Wrap the pancetta around the chicken. Repeat with the rest of the pancetta and chicken.

Put the wrapped chicken on top of the leeks and baste with some of the buttery leek juices.

Cook in the Remoska for **approx 20-30 minutes** (depending on the thickness of the chicken breasts) until the chicken is cooked.

Roast Chicken Dinner

Ingredients	Standard	Grand
Olive oil	1tbsp	2tbsp
Butter, melted	2tbsp	4tbsp
Grainy mustard	1tbsp	2tbsp
Honey	1tbsp	2tbsp
Carrot, sliced	1	2
Potato, large, chopped	1	2
Parsnip, sliced	1	2
Salt and pepper		
Lemon thyme sprigs	6	8
Poussin	1	2

Method

Mix together the oil, butter, mustard and honey. Toss the vegetables in half the mixture, add salt and pepper to taste and put into the Remoska with 4 sprigs lemon thyme.

Season the poussin with salt and pepper and put the remaining thyme sprigs inside.

Place on top of the vegetables and pour over the remaining oil mixture.

Cook in the Remoska for **approx 50-60 minutes**, until the vegetables are tender and the poussin is cooked through, with no pink juices.

Roast Pheasant

Ingredients	Standard
Pheasant, oven ready	1
Butter	50g
Bacon, streaky slices	3
Herbs: thyme, sage, rosemary, chopped	2-3tsp

Method

Rub the pheasant breast with the butter and cover with strips of bacon. Scatter over the herbs.

Put in a roasting bag. Place in the Remoska. Cook for **approx 45-60 minutes** according to the size of the bird. Serve on slices of hot fried bread with watercress or other vegetables.

Spanish Style Chicken

Ingredients	Standard	Grand
Chicken thighs, boneless, skinless	6	9
Flour, plain	2tbsp	3tbsp
Paprika, smoked	1tsp	3tsp
Olive oil	2tbsp	3tbsp
Onion, chopped	1	2
Peppers, red, chopped	2	3
Garlic cloves, crushed	1	2
Chorizo sausage, thickly sliced	125g	175g
Dry sherry	120ml	180ml
Stock, chicken, hot	200ml	300ml
Thyme sprigs	3-4	5-6

Method

Put the flour and paprika in a plastic food bag and toss the chicken thighs until coated.

Heat half the oil in a frying pan and quickly brown the chicken thighs. Remove from the pan and put into the Remoska.

Heat the remaining oil in the frying pan and cook the onion, peppers, garlic and chorizo for **approx 8-10 minutes** until softened. Pour in the sherry and bring to the boil.

Tip the contents of the pan into the Remoska and add the stock and thyme. Stir well and cook for **approx 40-45 minutes** until the chicken is cooked through and the vegetables are tender.

Spiced Chicken

Ingredients	Standard	Grand
Chicken	1.5-1.75kg	2kg
Butter	75g	110g
Cumin	$\frac{1}{2}$tsp	$\frac{3}{4}$tsp
Coriander seeds, crushed	2tsp	3tsp
Cardamom seeds, crushed	2tsp	3tsp
Pepper, black	$\frac{1}{2}$tsp	$\frac{3}{4}$tsp
Salt	1tsp	$1\frac{1}{2}$tsp
Ginger, fresh grated	2.5cm	5cm
Garlic clove, crushed	1	2
Lemon, zest	$\frac{1}{2}$	1
Juice of lemons	1	2

Method

Loosen the skin on the breast and legs of the chicken without breaking the skin. Cream the butter and beat in the spices, salt, pepper, ginger, garlic, lemon zest and juice. Pack the spiced butter under the skin to cover the breast and legs. Leave to stand for **up to 2 hours.**

Place the chicken into a roasting bag and cut a slit in the top of the bag. Place in the Remoska and cook for **40 minutes per kg, plus 20 minutes** until the chicken is cooked through.

Stuffed Chicken Breasts

Ingredients	Standard	Grand
Oil	1tbsp	2tbsp
Mushrooms, button	100g	150g
Chicken breasts, skinless, boneless	2	4
Salt and pepper		
Spinach, baby leaves	50g	75g
Tarragon, chopped	1tbsp	$1\frac{1}{2}$tbsp
Roasted pepper pieces from a jar, drained	4	8
Wine, white	65ml	95ml

Method

Put the oil in the Remoska and add the mushrooms. Cook in the Remoska while you prepare the chicken.

Slice the chicken breasts horizontally, almost, but not quite in half to make a pocket. Season with salt and pepper. Divide the spinach, tarragon and peppers between the pockets, then fold over the top half of the chicken.

Stir the mushrooms and put to one side of the Remoska. Place the chicken in the Remoska and drizzle with a little oil from the jar of peppers. Pour in the wine and cook for **approx 35-40 minutes** until the chicken is cooked through.

Stuffed Chicken Breasts with Pancetta

Ingredients	Standard	Grand
Chicken breasts, boneless	4	6
Breadcrumbs	4tbsp	6tbsp
Lemon, grated zest	1	2
Butter, melted	2tbsp	4tbsp
Pancetta, diced	70g	100g
Thyme, chopped	3tsp	5tsp
Cherry tomatoes, halved	6	9
Pancetta strips	8	12
Olive oil		

Method

Slice the chicken breasts horizontally, to make a pocket in each.

Mix the breadcrumbs, lemon zest, melted butter, diced pancetta and thyme until well combined. Spoon into the pockets in the chicken.

Place the tomatoes on top of the stuffing. Wrap 2 strips of pancetta around each chicken breast to fit tightly. The pancetta will shrink as it cooks.

Drizzle a little oil over the chicken breasts. Drizzle a little oil into the Remoska. Put the chicken into the Remoska and cook for **approx 30-40 minutes** (depending on the thickness of the chicken) until browned and sizzling.

tomato

Sweet and Sticky Chicken

Ingredients	Standard	Grand
Honey	2tbsp	3tbsp
Light soy sauce	4tbsp	6tbsp
Garlic clove, crushed	3tbsp	4½tbsp
Hoisin sauce	1	2
Stem ginger pieces, finely chopped	2	3
Ginger syrup from the jar	2tbsp	3tbsp
Star anise	2	3
Cinnamon stick, broken	1	1
Ginger root, grated	2tsp	3tsp
Chicken, thigh fillets	6	9

Method

Mix all the ingredients together, except the chicken.

Make cuts in each chicken thigh with a sharp knife. Add the chicken to the spice mixture and mix well until the chicken is coated. Cover and marinate for at least **4 hours** or overnight.

Put into the Remoska and cook for **approx 25-35 minutes** until the chicken is cooked through. Remove the whole spices and serve with boiled rice.

Tandoori Chicken

Ingredients	Standard	Grand
Yoghurt, plain	150ml	225ml
Garlic cloves, crushed	2	3
Ground cumin	1tsp	1½tsp
Turmeric	1tsp	1½tsp
Chilli powder	1tsp	1½tsp
Lemon, juice	1	1½
Ginger piece, grated	2.5cm	4cm
Salt	½tsp	¾tsp
Chicken thighs, skinless, boneless	6	9

Method

Mix together the yoghurt, garlic, spices and salt in a large shallow dish.

Score the chicken pieces with a sharp knife and put into the yoghurt mixture, turning to coat. Cover and leave to stand for **1 hour**, turning from time to time. Lift the chicken from the marinade and put into the Remoska.

Cook for **approx 20-30 minutes**, until the chicken is cooked through and there is no pink juice.

Thai Green Chicken Curry

Ingredients	Standard	Grand
Vegetable oil	1tbsp	1½tbsp
Thai green curry paste	2tbsp	3tbsp
Sugar	2tsp	3tsp
Chicken breasts, boneless, cut into chunks	450g	675g
Kaffir lime leaves, torn into pieces	3	5
Coconut milk	350ml	500ml
Thai fish sauce	2tsp	3tsp
Coriander handful, roughly chopped		
Lime juice to taste		

Method

Heat the oil in the Remoska. Add the green curry paste and sugar and cook for **5 minutes**, stirring. Stir in the chicken pieces and lime leaves, until coated in the paste.

Add the coconut milk and fish sauce and cook for **approx 20-30 minutes** until thickened slightly and the chicken is cooked through.

Stir in the coriander and lime juice to taste. Serve with boiled rice.

Turkey Olives

Ingredients	Standard
Turkey breast	500g
Salt and pepper	
Sun dried tomatoes	$\frac{3}{4}$ small jar
Artichoke hearts	$\frac{1}{2}$ jar
Worcestershire sauce	1tsp
Balsamic vinegar	1tsp
Tomato purée	1tsp
Wine, white	200ml

Method

Cut the turkey breast into long thin steaks and batten them out nice and flat. At one end place the tomatoes and the artichoke hearts, roll up and tie (not too tight) with string.

Place in the Remoska, mix all the remaining ingredients, pour over the turkey olives and cook for **approx 20 minutes**. Take out the turkey olives and reduce the sauce slightly for a **further 10 minutes**.

Venison Casserole

Ingredients	Grand
For the marinade:	
Olive oil	4tbsp
Red wine or sherry	2tbsp
Lemon rind, grated	1tsp
Nutmeg, freshly grated	$\frac{1}{2}$tsp
Juniper berries, crushed	1tbsp
Garlic clove, crushed	1
Salt and black pepper	

Combine all the ingredients of the marinade in a screw top jar and shake well.

Oil	2tbsp
Mushrooms, button	100g
Onion, large, sliced	1
Pepper, green, sliced	1
Carrots, sliced	4
Celery sticks, chopped	4
Garlic clove, crushed	1
Venison, cubed and marinated overnight	1kg
Gammon or bacon, diced	100g
Flour, plain	30g
Stock, chicken	275ml
Wine, red	75ml

Method

Fry the vegetables in a large pan to a good dark colour. Add the garlic, bacon and the marinated venison, stirring well. Add the flour, stir, add the wine and stock, stir and transfer to the Remoska.

Cook for **approx 1-1$\frac{1}{2}$ hours** until the meat is tender. This is best if left to cool, kept refrigerated overnight and heated the following day.

Meat

Beef and Haggis Meat Loaf

Ingredients	Standard	Grand
Beef, minced	500g	750g
Haggis	150g	200g
Tomato purée	4tbsp	6tbsp
Breadcrumbs, fresh	4tbsp	6tbsp
Eggs	1	2
Mustard	$\frac{1}{2}$tbsp	1tbsp
Salt and pepper to taste		

Method

Mix all the ingredients, using your hands until well blended. Form into a loaf shape, wrap in foil. Place in the Remoska and bake for **approx 1 hour** in the Standard or **1½ hours** in the Grand, depending on the size of the meatloaf.

Beef Potato Pie

Ingredients	Standard	Grand
Potatoes, peeled	500g	750g
Butter	75g	110g
Flour, plain	175g	250g
Salt and pepper		
Beef, lean minced	225g	450g
Horseradish sauce	2tbsp	4tbsp
Tomato purée	2tbsp	4tbsp
Tomato ketchup	$\frac{1}{2}$tbsp	1tbsp
Mustard, Dijon	1tbsp	1$\frac{1}{2}$tbsp
Sundried tomatoes in oil, drained	4	8

Method

Cook the potatoes in boiling salted water until tender. Drain and mash with the butter. Season to taste with salt and pepper. Stir in the flour and mix to a soft dough. Pat about two thirds of the potato dough onto the base of the Remoska.

Mix the minced beef with the horseradish sauce, tomato purée, ketchup and mustard and a sprinkling of salt and pepper until well blended.

Shape into a round the same size as the potato dough round and press lightly on top of the dough. Top with the sun-dried tomatoes.

Pat out the remaining dough and cut strips to fit across the top of the meat. Cook in the Remoska for **approx 40-50 minutes**, until the potato is brown and crisp and the mince is cooked through.

mustard

Beef Steaks in Foil Parcels

Ingredients	Standard	Grand
Beef steaks	2 x 225g	4 x 225g
Oil for brushing meat		
Salt and black pepper		
Mustard, German	1tsp	2tsp
Onion, medium size, sliced thinly	1	2
Cheese, Jarlsberg, grated	50g	100g
Tomato ketchup		

Method

Tenderise the steaks, brush with the oil and refrigerate for an hour.

Place each steak on a piece of foil, spread with the mustard, top with sliced onions, season to taste and seal to keep juices from escaping. Place in the Remoska and cook until tender, **approx 30-40 minutes.**

Carefully peel back the foil, top with cheese, drizzle with ketchup and cook until the cheese has melted, **approx 10-15 minutes.**

Egg, Chorizo and Cheese Puffs

Ingredients	Grand
Pastry, puff	225 g
Eggs	2
Cheese, Cheddar, grated	30g
Chorizo sausage, diced	40g

Method

Roll out the pastry and cut into 2 squares. Prick all over with a fork. Cook in the Remoska for **15 minutes** until puffed and pale gold.

Make a hollow in the centre of each square with a spoon and break an egg in the hollow. Sprinkle with cheese and chorizo.

Cook for **15 minutes** until the pastry is golden and the eggs are cooked.

chorizo

Ham and Sausage Casserole with Pearl Barley

Ingredients	Grand
Oil	1tbsp
Toulouse sausages	6
Ham hock, ready-cooked and cubed off the bone	1
Bacon, lardons	100g
Pearl barley	50g
Carrots, roughly chopped	4
Onions, roughly chopped	2
Leeks, roughly chopped	3
Potatoes, roughly chopped	4
Peppers, red, sliced	2
Bouquet garni	1
Salt and pepper	
Water	

Method

Heat the oil in the Remoska and brown the sausages on both sides. Add the remaining ingredients, season with salt and pepper and just cover with water.

Cook in the Remoska for **1 hour**, until the sausages and the vegetables are cooked.

Ladle into warm serving bowls.

Hot Beef Loaf

Ingredients	Standard	Grand
French baguette loaf, small	1	2
Oil	2tbsp	4tbsp
Onion, chopped, small	1	2
Beef, minced	350g	700g
Allspice	$\frac{1}{2}$tsp	1
Tomato purée	1tbsp	2
Salt and pepper		
Cream cheese with herbs and garlic	200g	400g
Parmesan cheese, grated	75g	150g

Method

Cut the loaf horizontally, keeping the 2 sides hinged together. Remove as much of the soft crumb as possible. You may need to cut off the end of the loaf to fit the Standard Remoska.

Heat 1 tablespoon oil in a frying pan and cook the onion for **3 minutes.** Add the beef and cook over a high heat until browned. Stir in the allspice and tomato purée and season to taste with salt and pepper. Simmer gently for **20 minutes.** Leave to cool.

Beat the cream cheese and spread over both halves of the loaf. Spoon the meat mixture into one half, pressing down well.

Sprinkle with the grated cheese and drizzle with the remaining oil. Close the loaf and wrap tightly in oiled foil.

Put into the Remoska and cook for **approx 30 minutes.** Leave to stand for **10 minutes,** then cut into thick slices.

Lamb Meatballs with Beans

Ingredients	Standard	Grand
Olive oil	2tbsp	3tbsp
Onion, chopped	1	2
Garlic cloves, chopped	2	5
Stock, lamb	400ml	600ml
Tomato purée	2tbsp	3tbsp
Salt and pepper		
Cannellini beans, drained	1 x 400g tin	2 x 400g tins
Butter beans	1 x 400g tin	2 x 400g tins
Rosemary	2-3 sprigs	3-4 sprigs
Bay leaf	1	2
For the meatballs:		
Lamb, minced	500g	750g
Egg, beaten	1	2
Breadcrumbs	50g	75g
Parsley, finely chopped	1tbsp	1½tbsp
Sage, chopped	1tsp	1½tsp
Salt and pepper		
Oil	2tbsp	3tbsp

Method

Heat the oil in a frying pan and cook the onion and garlic until translucent. Stir in the tomato purée, stock and beans and season to taste with salt and pepper.

Put into the Remoska with the rosemary and bay leaf.

For the meatballs: mix the lamb with the egg, breadcrumbs, parsley and sage. Season with salt and pepper and form into balls.

Heat the oil in a frying pan and fry the meatballs until browned on all sides.

Place the meatballs on top of the bean mixture. Switch on the Remoska and cook for **approx 30-35 minutes** until the meatballs are cooked through.

Lamb Shoulder with Peppers

Ingredients	Standard	Grand
Lamb, boneless shoulder	700g	1kg
Rosemary	2tbsp	3tbsp
Oregano	1tbsp	1½tbsp
Thyme	1tbsp	1½tbsp
Garlic cloves	4	6
Olive oil		
Salt and pepper		
Peppers, sliced	2	4
Lemon, thickly sliced	1	2
Spring onions, chopped	5	8

Method

Pound the herbs, and garlic with a little olive oil to a coarse paste. Season with a little salt and pepper.

Lay the lamb skin side down and spread with the paste. Roll up the lamb and secure with a skewer or tie with cotton string.

Put the peppers, lemon and spring onions into a roasting bag with the lamb on top. Tie the bag and cut a slit in the top.

Cook in the Remoska for **approx 60-70 minutes** (Standard) or **approx 80-90 minutes** (Grand), until the lamb is cooked to your liking.

Slice the lamb and serve with the peppers and lemon slices.

Lamb Stuffed Aubergines

Ingredients	Standard	Grand
Oil	2tbsp	3tbsp
Aubergines	2	4
Onion, finely chopped	1	2
Garlic clove, finely chopped	2	3
Lamb, mince	250g	450g
Ground allspice	1tsp	2tsp
Ground coriander	1tsp	2tsp
Salt and pepper		
Sun-dried tomatoes in oil, drained	6	8

Method

Using a sharp knife slit each aubergine lengthways down the middle to form a pocket - don't cut through the ends or the base.

Heat the oil in a frying pan. Fry the aubergines for **approx 5 minutes** turning on all sides, until starting to soften. Remove with a slotted spoon. Add the onions and garlic to the pan and fry until softened. Leave to cool.

Mix the minced lamb with the spices, onions and garlic. Season to taste with salt and pepper. Stuff the lamb filling into each aubergine and place 3 slices of sun-dried tomato on top of each one.

Put into the Remoska and drizzle with a little oil from the jar of sun-dried tomatoes. Cook for **approx 40-45 minutes** until the aubergines are tender and the lamb is cooked through.

Lamb with Herb Stuffing

Ingredients	Standard	Grand
Mint and rosemary, freshly chopped	2tbsp	3tbsp
Breadcrumbs, fresh	50g	75g
Egg yolk, beaten	1	2
Salt and ground black pepper		
Lemon, finely grated zest	1	2
Lamb leg, boned (butterflied)	450g	700-900g
Roasting bag		
For the topping:		
Mustard, Dijon	2tbsp	3-4tbsp
Sugar, Demerara	1tbsp	2tbsp

Method

Mix together the herbs, breadcrumbs, salt and black pepper and the lemon rind until well combined and bind with the egg yolk. Leave to stand for **5 minutes.**

Lay the lamb flat on a work surface and using a sharp knife cut a pocket through the centre. Place the stuffing in the pocket and roll the meat together and secure with string.

For the topping: mix together the mustard and sugar and spread over the lamb.

Place in the roasting bag, tie securely and place in the Remoska. Cook for **approx 1 hour** for the Standard and **approx 1-1¾ hours** for the Grand, until the lamb is tender.

mint

Minced Beef Wellington

Ingredients	Standard	Grand
Beef, minced	500g	750g
Tomato ketchup	2tbsp	3tbsp
Eggs	2	3
Mustard, Dijon	2tbsp	3tbsp
Salt	$\frac{1}{2}$tsp	$\frac{3}{4}$tsp
Freshly ground black pepper	$\frac{1}{2}$tsp	$\frac{3}{4}$tsp
Pastry, puff	500g	700g

Method

Mix the beef with the ketchup, 1 egg, 1 tablespoon mustard, salt and pepper. Shape the meat into a flat oval shape to fit the Remoska. Cook in the Remoska for **20 minutes** then remove and switch off the Remoska.

Roll the pastry into a rectangle large enough to wrap up the beef. Beat the remaining egg and brush over pastry. Spread the mustard along the middle of the pastry. Place the meat on top then fold the pastry over the meat to make a parcel. Trim off any excess pastry. (Use the trimmings to make pastry leaves).

Brush with beaten egg, make a slit in the top and decorate with pastry leaves. Put into the Remoska and cook for **approx 30-40 minutes**, until the pastry is puffed, crisp and golden.

One Pot Lamb Curry with Rice

Ingredients	Standard	Grand
Lamb neck fillet, cubed	500g	750g
Salt and pepper		
Oil	1tbsp	2tbsp
Onion, chopped	1	2
Curry paste	3-4tbsp	5-6tbsp
Stock, lamb	450ml	670ml
Tomatoes, canned, chopped	400g	600g
Cinnamon stick, broken	1	2
Garlic cloves, crushed	3	5
Root ginger, grated	1½tbsp	3tbsp
Potato, large, diced	1	2
Basmati rice	150g	225g

Method

Season the lamb with salt and pepper. Heat the oil in a frying pan and brown the lamb in batches. Transfer to a bowl.

Add the onion to the pan and cook for **5 minutes**. Put into the bowl with the lamb and stir in the curry paste. Put the lamb and onion into the Remoska and stir in the stock, tomatoes, cinnamon sticks, garlic and ginger.

Cook in the Remoska for **30 minutes**. Add the potato and cook for **10 minutes**. Stir in the rice and cook for a **further 15-20 minutes**, until the rice is cooked and most of the liquid has been absorbed. If the mixture seems too dry during the last stage of cooking add more hot stock or hot water.

Pigs in Cheese Blankets

Ingredients	Standard	Grand
Oil	1 tbsp	1½ tbsp
Sausages	6	9
Pastry, puff	300g	400g
Cheese, Cheddar, grated	110g	175g

Method

Heat the oil in a frying pan and brown the sausages on all sides. Remove and leave to cool.

Roll out the pastry into a large square on a lightly floured surface. Cut the pastry sheet in half.

Sprinkle one half with the grated cheese and place the other pastry sheet on top. Dampen the edges and roll out again, to enclose the cheese.

Cut the pastry into 6 lengths (9 for the Grand) and wrap a length around each sausage. Place in the Remoska and cook for **approx 30-40 minutes** until the sausages are cooked through and the pastry is golden.

Sausage and Bacon Bake with Cheese Crust

Ingredients	Standard	Grand
Oil	1 tbsp	1½ tbsp
Sausages, thickly sliced	3	6
Bacon rashers, cut into strips	2	4
Tomatoes, quartered	2	4
Breadcrumbs, fresh	2 tbsp	4 tbsp
Cheese, Cheddar, grated	75g	110g

Method

Heat the oil in the Remoska and cook the sausages for **approx 15 minutes** until browned. Add the bacon and tomatoes to the Remoska and cook for a **further 15 minutes**.

Sprinkle with the breadcrumbs and cheese and cook for a **further 10-15 minutes** until the top is bubbling and golden.

Sausage Puff

Ingredients	Standard
Pastry, puff	375g
Mustard, Dijon	1tbsp
Oil	1tbsp
Onion, small, finely chopped	1
Sausage meat	900g
Egg for brushing	

Method

Roll out the pastry into a rectangle and brush with the mustard, leaving a border around the edges.

Heat the oil in the Remoska and cook the onion for **approx 15 minutes** until soft. Put into a bowl and mix in the sausage meat.

Put the sausage mixture down the middle length of the pastry. With a sharp knife cut slits 3cm apart, about $\frac{1}{2}$cm away from the sausage mixture. Brush with beaten egg.

Fold the slit pastry over the sausage meat and brush again with beaten egg.

Cook in the Remoska for **approx 50-60 minutes** until the pastry is golden and the sausage meat is cooked through.

Sausages with Apple and Red Onion

Ingredients	Standard	Grand
Oil	1tbsp	2tbsp
Sausages	8	10-12
Onions, red, cut into wedges	3	5
Garlic cloves, chopped	2	4
Flour, plain	1tbsp	2tbsp
Wine, red	100ml	150ml
Stock, vegetable	200ml	350ml
Tomato purée	2tsp	4tsp
Apples, cooking	3	5
Salt and pepper		

Method

Heat the oil in a frying pan and brown the sausages, but don't cook them. Put the sausages into the Remoska. Add the onions to the pan and fry for **approx 5 minutes** until soft. Add the garlic and fry for **1 minute** to soften.

Sprinkle the flour over and stir until thick. Remove from the heat and stir in the wine, stock and tomato purée and season with salt and pepper. Put the mixture into the Remoska.

Core the apples and cut into wedges. Place in the Remoska.

Cook for **approx 30-35 minutes**, until the sausages are cooked and the apples are soft.

Spiced Roast Pork with Fruit

Ingredients	Standard	Grand
Flour	1tbsp	2tbsp
Allspice, ground	1tsp	2tsp
Cinnamon, ground	$\frac{1}{2}$tsp	1tsp
Peppercorns		
Salt		
Rolled pork loin, boneless joint	1kg	2kg
Apples, dried	175g	225g
Pears, dried	175g	225g
Prunes	110g	175g
Sugar	50g	75g
Orange juice	150ml	300ml

Method

Place the flour, spices and a few peppercorns in a roasting bag and shake well to coat.

Rub the pork rind with a little salt. Place the pork and dried fruits in the bag, sprinkle in the sugar and pour in the orange juice. Tie the bag securely and cook for **approx 1$\frac{1}{2}$-1$\frac{3}{4}$ hours** for the Standard and **approx 1$\frac{1}{2}$-2 hours** for the Grand, until the pork is cooked through.

If the pork is browning too quickly, cover with a double layer of foil.

Remove from the Remoska, carefully cut open the bag and place the meat on a heated serving plate. Arrange the dried fruits around the pork and spoon the juices over the pork and fruit.

cinnamon

Sticky Sausages

Ingredients	Standard	Grand
Oil	1tbsp	2tbsp
Sausages	6-8	10-12
Sugar, dark muscovado	110g	150g
Lemon juice	50ml	75ml
Sherry or ginger wine	3tbsp	5tbsp
Marmalade, Seville or Bitter Orange	3tbsp	5tbsp
Garlic cloves, crushed	2	3
Soy sauce	2tbsp	3tbsp
Pepper, white, to taste		

Method

Heat the oil in a frying pan and brown the sausages on all sides. Drain off the fat and put the sausages into the Remoska. Put the remaining ingredients into a pan over a low heat and stir until the sugar has dissolved completely. Increase the heat, bring to the boil and cook for **2 minutes.**

Pour the sauce over the sausages, cook for **10 minutes,** baste the sausages and further cook for **approx 20 minutes.**

Good with creamy mashed potatoes.

Stuffed Lamb Chops with Peppers

Ingredients	Standard	Grand
Peppers, seeds removed and sliced	2	3
Onion, chopped	1	2
Olive oil	1tbsp	1½tbsp
Lamb chops	4	6
Salt and pepper		
Rosemary, chopped	4tsp	6tsp
Thyme	4tsp	6tsp
Mustard, Dijon	4tsp	6tsp
Rosemary sprigs	2	3
Vinegar, Balsamic	1tbsp	1½tbsp

Method

Toss the peppers and onion in the oil and put into the Remoska. Cook while you prepare the chops.

Slice the chops horizontally into the meat and fat to make a pocket. Season with salt and pepper.

Mix together the rosemary, thyme and mustard and push into the pockets in the chops. Push half a rosemary sprig into the pockets.

Place on top of the peppers and onions and drizzle with the vinegar. Cook for **approx 30-40 minutes**, depending on the thickness of the chops.

Teviotdale Pie

Ingredients	Standard	Grand
Oil	1tbsp	2tbsp
Lamb, lean, minced	450g	675g
Onion, chopped	1	2
Stock, beef	300 ml	450ml
Thyme	2tsp	3tsp
Salt and pepper		
Flour, self-raising	225g	350g
Cornflour	25g	55g
Suet, shredded	75g	130g
Milk	300ml	450ml

Method

Heat the oil in a frying pan and cook the lamb for a **few minutes** until beginning to brown. Add the onion and continue to cook for **another 5 minutes** until soft. Stir in the stock and thyme. Season to taste and put into the Remoska. Cook for **20 minutes.**

Put the flour, cornflour and suet in a mixing bowl and gradually beat in the milk to form a thick batter. Season well with salt and pepper. Spoon the batter over the meat mixture and continue to cook for **approx 30-35 minutes** until risen and golden.

Fish

Fish Parcels

Ingredients	Standard	Grand
Plaice fillets	4	6
Salt and pepper		
Lemon juice	4tbsp	6tbsp
Cider	4tbsp	6tbsp
Parsley, chopped	4tbsp	6tbsp
Thyme sprigs	4	6
Tomatoes, sliced	4	6

Method

Cut 4 x 30cm squares of non-stick baking paper. Place a fish fillet in the centre of each square.

Sprinkle each fillet with salt and pepper, 1 tablespoon lemon juice and 1 tablespoon cider, followed by 1 tablespoon parsley. Add a sprig of thyme to each parcel. Arrange the sliced tomatoes over each fillet, overlapping them.

Fold in the edges of the paper to enclose completely the filling and form a parcel. Place the parcels in the Remoska and bake for **approx 15-20 minutes** (depending on the thickness of the fish) until the fish is cooked.

Fish with Olive and Tomato Crust

Ingredients	Standard	Grand
Fish fillets, white	2	4
Black olives, pitted	35g	70g
Olive oil	1½tbsp	3tbsp
Salt	¼tsp	½tsp
Black pepper, ground	¼tsp	½tsp
Lemon juice	1tbsp	2tbsp
Cherry tomatoes	6-8	12

Method

Put the fish in the Remoska.

Blend the remaining ingredients, except the cherry tomatoes, in a food processor to a paste and spread evenly over the fish.

Bake for **approx 20-25 minutes,** until the fish is cooked and the topping is lightly browned.

Add the cherry tomatoes for the last **10 minutes** of cooking.

tomatoes

Fishcakes

Ingredients	Standard	Grand
Haddock fillets, skinless	350g	500g
Potatoes, large	3	5
Butter	25g	50g
Parsley	2tbsp	3tbsp
Salt and pepper		

Method

Poach or steam the fish until cooked, then flake into pieces.

Cook the potatoes in boiling salted water until tender. Mash with the butter until smooth. Add the parsley and flaked fish and season to taste with salt and pepper. Set aside to cool.

Brush a little oil on the base of the Remoska.

Shape the mixture into fishcakes, 4 for the Standard (6 for the Grand), and put into the Remoska. Brush the tops with oil.

Cook for **approx 20 minutes** until golden brown.

Haddock with Lemon Butter Sauce

Ingredients	Standard	Grand
Haddock fillets	2	4
Salt		
Butter, melted	2tbsp	4tbsp
Lemon juice	2tbsp	4tbsp
Lemon, cut into wedges	1	2
Caper berries, rinsed	1tbsp	2tbsp

Method

Place the fish in the Remoska. Season to taste with salt.

Drizzle over half the butter and all the lemon juice.

Put the lemon wedges in the Remoska. Place the caper berries on top of the haddock and drizzle with the remaining butter.

Cook for **approx 20 minutes** (depending on the thickness of the fish) until cooked through.

capers

Halibut Bake

Ingredients	Standard	Grand
Butter for Remoska		
Halibut steaks	2 x 225g	4 x 225g
Cider, dry	150ml	300ml
Herbs, finely chopped:		
parsley, thyme, rosemary		
and tarragon	1tbsp	2tbsp

Method

Butter the Remoska and place the halibut steaks in the Remoska.

Mix the herbs with the cider, pour over the fish and cook **approx 15-20 minutes** until the fish will flake easily.

Macaroni and Tuna Bake

Ingredients	Standard	Grand
Macaroni	400g	600g
Butter	55g	75g
Flour, plain	50g	75g
Milk	600ml	900ml
Cheese, Cheddar, grated	200g	300g
Tuna	2 x 160g cans	3 x 160g cans
Sweet corn	300g	450g
Salt and pepper		

Method

Cook the macaroni for **2 minutes** less time than stated on the packet. Drain well.

Melt the butter in a pan and stir in the flour. Cook for **1 minute,** then gradually stir in the milk to make a thick sauce. Remove from the heat and stir in most of the cheese.

Drain the pasta; mix with the sauce, tuna and sweet corn. Season to taste with salt and pepper.

Put into the Remoska and sprinkle with the remaining grated cheese.

Cook for **approx 25-30 minutes** until golden and bubbling.

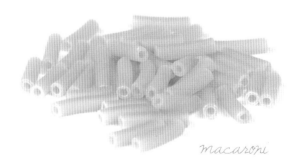

macaroni

Mediterranean Salmon

Ingredients	Standard	Grand
Yellow pepper, cut into strips	1	2
Courgette, sliced	1	2
Onion, cut into wedges	1	2
Tomatoes, cherry	200g	400g
Garlic cloves, chopped	2	4
Thyme, chopped	1tbsp	2tbsp
Oil	3tbsp	5tbsp
Lemon juice	2tbsp	4tbsp
Stock, vegetable	100ml	200ml
Fennel seeds	2tsp	4tsp
Salmon fillets	2	4
Salt and freshly ground pepper		

Method

Put the vegetables into the Remoska and season with salt and pepper. Sprinkle with the thyme, oil and half the lemon juice. Pour in the stock and scatter in the fennel seeds. Cook for **20 minutes.**

Stir the vegetables and place the salmon fillets on top. Sprinkle with the remaining lemon juice and season with salt and pepper.

Continue cooking for a **further 15 minutes** until the salmon is cooked through and the vegetables are tender.

Oriental Salmon

Ingredients	Standard	Grand
Salmon fillets	2	4
Olive oil	2tbsp	4tbsp
Soy sauce	2tbsp	4tbsp
Honey	2tbsp	4tbsp
Bergamot, unwaxed,		
(or lime) grated zest and juice	1	$1\frac{1}{2}$
Spring onions, cut into strips	4	8

Method

Put the salmon fillets in a bowl.

Mix together the oil, soy sauce, honey, bergamot zest and juice. Pour over the salmon and turn to coat. Cover and leave to stand for **1 hour.**

Tip into the Remoska with the marinade. Add the spring onions and cook for **approx 20-25 minutes,** depending on the thickness of the salmon until the salmon is cooked through.

Salmon in Couscous Parcels

Ingredients	Standard	Grand
Couscous	110g	225g
Stock, vegetable, hot	200ml	400ml
Oil	1tbsp	2tbsp
Thyme, chopped	1tbsp	2tbsp
Spring onion, chopped	4	6
Sun-blush tomatoes, chopped	4	6
Salt and pepper to taste		
Salmon fillets approx 150g each	2	4

Method

Put the couscous into a bowl, stir in the hot stock and the oil. Cover with cling film and leave to stand for **10 minutes.** Fluff up with a fork, add the thyme, spring onions and tomatoes and season to taste.

Divide the mixture onto 2 or 4 large sheets of foil. Place the salmon fillet on top of the couscous and lightly season. Fold the foil to form a parcel and place in the Remoska. Cook for **approx 20 minutes.**

Salmon with Lime and Pancetta

Ingredients	Standard
Salmon steaks	4 x 125g
Limes, thinly sliced	2
Pancetta, finely sliced	100g
Salt and pepper	

Method

Season the salmon, lay 4-5 slices of lime on top of the salmon steaks.

Wrap each slice in 3-4 slices of the pancetta.

Place in the Remoska and cook for **approx 12-15 minutes** depending on the thickness of the salmon.

spring onions

Salmon with Peppers and Lemon

Ingredients	Standard	Grand
Salmon fillets	2	4
Salt and pepper		
Spring onions, sliced	4	8
Peppers, deseeded, chopped	2	4
Lemon, juice, grated zest	1	2
Wine, white	4tbsp	8tbsp

Method

Season the salmon with salt and pepper.

Put the spring onions and peppers in a roasting bag. Place the salmon fillets on top, followed by the lemon juice and zest and then pour over the wine.

Seal the bag, cut a slit in the top and cook in the Remoska for **approx 15-20 minutes,** until the vegetables are tender and the salmon is cooked through.

Trout Baked with Almonds

Ingredients	Standard
Trout, small	2
Lemon, juice	1
Salt and pepper	
Flour, plain, seasoned (for coating)	
Oil	2tbsp
Almonds, sliced	50g
Butter	2tbsp
Lemon	1
Parsley or chives, chopped	2tbsp

Method

Drizzle the trout with lemon juice and season. Dust with seasoned flour and place in a small amount of hot oil in the Remoska. Cook on both sides for **approx 5-10 minutes.**

Meanwhile dry fry the almonds in a frying pan until lightly brown. Place the trout on a plate, top with melted and browned butter (heated in a small pan until brown, but taking care not to burn it). Sprinkle the trout with almonds and garnish with lemon wedges, chopped parsley or chives.

Serve with potatoes and vegetables.

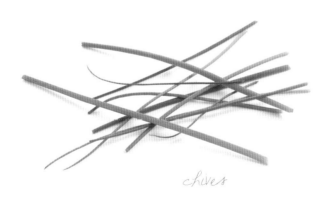

chives

Pasta
& Rice

Baked Pasta Pots

Ingredients	Standard	Grand
Fresh lasagna sheets	6	9
Tomato passata	500g	750g
Cheese, Cheddar, grated	200g	300g
Thyme, chopped	1tbsp	1½tbsp
Olive oil		
Cheese, Parmesan, grated	50g	75g

Method

Pour boiling water over the lasagna sheets and leave for **1 minute**. Drain well.

Cut rounds from the lasagna sheets, to line 4 small pie or tart moulds (6 for the Grand) and 4 rounds (6 for the Grand) for the top.

Spoon on the passata and sprinkle with cheese and thyme. Repeat the layers until the moulds are full.

Place the lasagna rounds on top, pressing the edges to seal. Brush the tops with oil and sprinkle with Parmesan.

Cook in the Remoska for **approx 35-40 minutes** until golden and bubbling.

Leave to stand for **5 minutes** and then turn out onto serving plates.

parmesan

Broccoli and Pasta Bake

Ingredients	Standard	Grand
Penne	225g	335g
Tomato pasta sauce, jar	500g	750g
Broccoli florets	300g	450g
Haricot beans, tin, drained	300g	450g
Cheese, Cheddar, grated	55g	85g
Breadcrumbs	60g	90g

Method

Put the penne in the Remoska and add the pasta sauce. Fill the jar almost to the top with water and add to the penne. Stir until mixed, cook for **20 minutes.**

Cook the broccoli in a pan of boiling salted water for **2 minutes** then drain well. Stir the broccoli and beans into the pasta.

Sprinkle the cheese and breadcrumbs over the top and cook for a **further 25 minutes** until golden brown.

Broken Pasta

Ingredients	Standard	Grand
Olive oil	2tbsp	3tbsp
Onion, finely chopped	1	2
Spaghetti or thin pasta	200g	300g
Tomatoes, tin, chopped	400g	600g
Olives	2tbsp	3tbsp
Caper berries, rinsed	1tbsp	1½tbsp
Wine, dry white	4tbsp	6tbsp
Boiling water	100-150ml	150-225ml
Salt and pepper		

Method

Heat the oil in the Remoska and cook the onion until softened.

Break the pasta in half lengthwise and add to the Remoska.

Stir in the tomatoes, olives and caper berries until well mixed. Cook for **10 minutes**.

Stir in the wine and water and cook for **approx 25-30 minutes**, adding more water if needed, until the pasta is soft. Season to taste with salt and pepper.

pasta

Chicken and Mushroom Pasta

Ingredients	Standard	Grand
Mushrooms, dried porcini	30g	45g
Chicken, skinless thighs	6	9
Salt and pepper		
Oil	2tbsp	3tbsp
Garlic cloves, crushed	2	3
Mushrooms, sliced	250g	375g
Wine, white	100ml	150ml
Bouquet garni		
Pasta	400g	600g
Cream, double	200ml	300ml

Method

Put the dried mushrooms in a small bowl and cover with boiling water. Leave to soak while you prepare the rest of the ingredients.

Season the chicken with salt and pepper. Heat the oil in the Remoska and brown the chicken on both sides.

Strain the porcini (reserve the soaking water) and add to the Remoska with the garlic, bouquet garni and fresh mushrooms.

Add the wine and soaking liquid and cook in the Remoska for **approx 30 minutes,** until the chicken is cooked through.

Meanwhile cook the pasta in a pan of boiling salted water according to the packet instructions. Drain well and season with salt and pepper. Add the drained pasta and the cream to the Remoska and stir well. Serve immediately.

Corn Spoonbread

Ingredients	Standard	Grand
Milk	400 ml	600ml
Yellow cornmeal (polenta)	110g	175g
Sugar	1tbsp	1½tbsp
Pepper	½tsp	¾tsp
Salt	½tsp	¾tsp
Butter, melted	2tbsp	3tbsp
Eggs, beaten	4	6

Method

Pour most of the milk into a pan and bring to the boil.

Whisk together the remaining milk and the cornmeal. Whisking constantly, slowly add the mixture to the boiling milk. Reduce the heat and simmer gently, stirring frequently, for **3 minutes.**

Remove from the heat and allow to cool slightly. Beat in the remaining ingredients and pour into the Remoska. Cook for **approx 30 minutes** until golden, risen and set. Serve warm.

Gnocchi Bake

Ingredients	Standard	Grand
Oil	2tbsp	3tbsp
Mushrooms, sliced	100g	150g
Gnocchi	500g	750g
Garlic clove, finely chopped	1	2
Spinach, baby	100g	150g
Yoghurt, plain	3tbsp	5tbsp
Salt and pepper		
Cheese, strong Cheddar, grated	75g	150g

Method

Heat the oil in the Remoska and cook the mushrooms. Meanwhile cook the gnocchi in a large pan of boiling salted water for **2 minutes**.

Add the garlic to the mushrooms in the Remoska.

Drain the gnocchi very well and carefully mix with the spinach, yoghurt and half the cheese. Season to taste with salt and pepper.

Put into the Remoska and stir gently with the mushrooms and garlic. Sprinkle with the remaining cheese and cook in the Remoska for **approx 20-25 minutes** until golden and bubbling.

Mince, Rice and Tomato Bake

Ingredients	Standard	Grand
Olive oil	1tbsp	1½tbsp
Onion, finely chopped	1	1 large
Garlic clove, finely chopped	1	2
Beef, minced	500g	750g
Tomatoes, tin, chopped	400g	600g
Stock, beef	250ml	375ml
Tomato purée	2tbsp	3tbsp
Oregano	2tsp	3tsp
Rice, Arborio	225g	350g
Cheese, Gruyère, grated	100g	150g

Method

Heat the oil in the Remoska and cook the onions and garlic for **approx 10 minutes** until softened.

Add the mince and cook until the meat is browned.

Add the tomatoes, beef stock, tomato purée, herbs and rice and stir to combine. Cook in the Remoska for **35 minutes**.

Sprinkle the cheese over the top and cook for a **further 20 minutes** until all the liquid is absorbed and the cheese is lightly browned. You may need to add more stock or water if the mixture is too dry.

Mushroom Rice

Ingredients	Standard	Grand
Olive oil	1½tbsp	2tbsp
Butter	25g	40g
Mushrooms, sliced	200g	300g
Garlic clove, finely chopped	1	2
Onion, finely chopped	1	1 large
Rice, Arborio	300g	450g
Sun-dried tomatoes, chopped	100g	150g
Stock, vegetable	400ml	600ml
Sherry	1tbsp	1½tbsp
Salt and pepper		

Method

Heat the oil and butter in the Remoska and cook the mushrooms, garlic and onion for **approx 10-15 minutes,** until softened.

Stir in the rice until coated with oil. Stir in the tomatoes, stock and sherry. Season to taste with salt and pepper.

Cook in the Remoska for **approx 25-30 minutes** until the liquid is absorbed.

mushrooms

Pasta Timbale

Ingredients	Standard	Grand
Pasta, Tortiglioni	250g	325g
Oil	3tbsp	4tbsp
Leeks, sliced	3	5
Pancetta, diced	80g	120g
Garlic cloves, crushed	2	3
Lemon thyme	1tbsp	2tbsp
Eggs	3	4
Egg yolk	1	2
Cream, whipping	300ml	450ml
Milk	150ml	225ml
Boursin minis	120g	180g
Salt and pepper		
Cheese, Parmesan, grated	75g	110g

Method

Cook the pasta in boiling salted water until almost, but not quite cooked. Drain and set aside.

Heat 2 tablespoons oil (3 for the Grand) in a frying pan and cook the leeks for **approx 5 minutes** until starting to soften. Add the pancetta, garlic and thyme and cook for **2 minutes.**

Whisk the eggs, egg yolk, cream, milk and salt and pepper. Stir in the Boursin minis and half the Parmesan. Stir in the leek mixture and drained pasta.

Put into the Remoska and press well down. Scatter with the remaining Parmesan. Drizzle with the remaining oil.

Cook in the Remoska for **approx 25-30 minutes** until set and golden.

101

Polenta Pizza with Peppers

Ingredients	Standard	Grand
Stock, vegetable	500ml	750ml
Thyme	1tsp	$1\frac{1}{2}$tsp
Polenta	175g	250g
Cheese, Gruyère, grated	175g	250g
Olive oil	2tbsp	3tbsp
Onion, finely chopped	1	2
Garlic cloves, crushed	2	3
Red pepper, diced	2	3
Oregano	1tbsp	$1\frac{1}{2}$tbsp
Salt and pepper		

Method

Heat the vegetable stock and thyme in a pan and bring to the boil. Add the polenta and cook, stirring, for **10 minutes,** until thick. Remove from the heat and stir in half the cheese until melted. Place in the Remoska, smoothing evenly to cover the base.

Heat the oil in a frying pan and cook the onion, garlic and peppers until just softened. Stir in the oregano, salt and pepper and cook for **3 minutes.**

Spoon on top of the polenta and sprinkle with the remaining cheese. Cook for **approx 25-30 minutes** until the cheese is melted and bubbling and the edges are browned.

pepper

Remoska Risotto

Ingredients	Standard	Grand
Pancetta, diced	500ml	750ml
Onion, chopped	1tsp	1½tsp
Garlic, clove, crushed	175g	250g
Mushrooms, chopped	175g	250g
Rice, Arborio	2tbsp	3tbsp
Stock, chicken or vegetable	200ml	300ml
Wine, white	2tbsp	3tbsp
Salt and pepper		
Cheese, Parmesan, grated	1tbsp	1½tbsp

Method

Cook the pancetta in the Remoska until the fat starts to run. Add the onion, garlic and mushrooms and cook for **approx 7-8 minutes** until softened and the pancetta is browned.

Stir in the rice, until coated in fat and cook for **2 minutes.**

Pour in the stock and leave to cook for **approx 30 minutes,** stirring once or twice until the rice is tender and all the stock is absorbed.

Season to taste with salt and pepper and serve topped with grated Parmesan cheese.

Spiced Rice Pilau

Ingredients	Standard	Grand
Olive oil	2tbsp	3tbsp
Onion, chopped	1	1 large
Garlic cloves, chopped	2	3
Turmeric	1tsp	1½tsp
Cinnamon sticks, broken	2	3
Cardamom pods, lightly crushed	3	5
Coriander seeds, lightly crushed	1tsp	1½tsp
Curry paste	1tsp	1½tsp
Bay leaves	2	3
Rice, Basmati	175g	260g
Stock, vegetable or chicken	400ml	600ml
Salt and pepper		

Method

Heat the oil in the Remoska and cook the onion and garlic for
15 minutes. Add the spices and bay leaves and cook for **3 minutes**.

Stir in the rice and cook for **2 minutes**.

Add the stock, stir and cook for **approx 25-30 minutes** until the stock is
absorbed. Fluff with a fork and season to taste with salt and pepper.

rice

Turkish Pilaf

Ingredients	Grand
Onion, large, finely chopped	1
Butter	65g
Rice, long grain, white or brown	250g
Cinnamon	$\frac{1}{2}$tsp
Allspice	$\frac{1}{4}$tsp
Mace	$\frac{1}{4}$tsp
Cloves, powdered	pinch
Stock, chicken or beef	900ml
Salt and black pepper to taste	
Nuts, pinenuts, pistachio or slivered almonds, mixed	60g
Currants	40g

Method

Fry the onion in the Remoska in half the butter until transparent. This takes **approx 10 minutes** with an occasional stir. Stir in the rice and cook for **5 minutes**. Add the spices and stock, stir well and cook until the liquid is absorbed, **approx 20 minutes**.

Meanwhile in a frying pan sauté the nuts and currants in the rest of the butter and stir into the rice when the rice is cooked. Good with lamb or chicken dishes.

Cheese

Camembert Baked in its Box

Ingredients   *Standard and Grand*

**One box of Camembert
still in its box packaging**

A small glass of white wine

Method

Remove the pine lid and the waxed paper from the Camembert. Wrap the outside of the box in aluminium foil and pour a small glass of white wine over the cheese.

For a crusty top, bake uncovered or for a softer top cover with foil. Place in the Remoska for **approx 15-20 minutes**, until the cheese is melted and bubbling.

Serve with fresh crusty bread or jacket potatoes, accompanied by a crisp green salad or green vegetables.

Cheese and Pancetta Pinwheels

Ingredients	Standard and Grand
Flour, self-raising	250g
Salt, pinch	
Butter	100g
Milk	120ml
Pancetta, diced	75g
Onion, finely chopped	1
Cream cheese with herbs and garlic	100g
Cheese, Cheddar, grated	100g

Method

Mix the flour and salt together in a mixing bowl. Rub in the butter until the mixture resembles breadcrumbs. Gradually add the milk (you may not need all of it) and mix to a dough. Roll out the dough on a floured surface to a rectangle about 1cm thick.

Mix together the pancetta, onion and both cheeses and spread over the dough, leaving a 2cm margin at the edges. Brush one long edge with water and roll up the dough into a roll, sealing the edges well.

Cut into 10-12 slices and place, cut side up in the Remoska.

Cook (4-5 at a time in the Standard 6-8 at a time in the Grand) for **approx 20-25 minutes** until golden and the filling is bubbling.

Serve warm.

cheese

Cheese and Parsley Gougères

Ingredients	Grand
Water	200ml
Butter	100g
Flour, plain	150g
Salt	½tbsp
Eggs	4
Cheese, Cheddar, grated	170g
Parsley, chopped	2tbsp

Method

Heat the water and butter in a large pan and bring to a boil. Tip in the flour and salt and mix well over a low heat until the mixture forms a ball that leaves the sides of the pan clean. Cool for a few minutes.

Beat in the eggs, one at a time until well blended and smooth. Beat in the cheese and parsley.

Drop spoonfuls of the mixture around the sides of the Remoska.

Cook for **approx 30-35 minutes** until golden brown and puffy.

Cheese and Thyme Puddings

Ingredients	Standard	Grand
Milk	200ml	300ml
Bay leaf	1	1
Butter	25g	50g
Flour, plain	20g	45g
Cheese, mature Cheddar, grated	75g	150g
Mustard, Dijon	½tsp	1tsp
Salt and pepper		
Eggs, medium, separated	2	3
Thyme	½tbsp	1tbsp
Cheese, Parmesan, grated	1tbsp	2tbsp

Method

Heat the milk and bay leaf in a pan and bring to the boil. Remove from the heat, cover and leave to stand for **15 minutes**. Melt the butter in a pan, add the flour and stir to a paste. Remove from the heat and stir in the milk. Remove the bay leaf.

Beat well and return to the heat and cook for **2 minutes**, stirring until thick. Remove from the heat and stir in the Cheddar cheese and mustard. Season to taste with salt and pepper. Set aside to cool slightly.

Whisk the egg whites until stiff. Beat the egg yolks and thyme into the cheese sauce, and then gradually fold in the egg whites until well blended.

Spoon into 2 greased 200ml ramekins or ovenproof dishes (4 for the Grand) and sprinkle with Parmesan. Place in the Remoska. Pour in boiling water to come halfway up the sides of the ramekins.

Cook for **approx 15-20 minutes** until risen and lightly golden.

thyme

Cheese, Potato and Vegetable Cake

Ingredients	Standard
Potatoes	500g
Cheese, Quark or Ricotta	125g
Vegetables, mixed frozen	100g
Egg	1
Cheese, Cheddar, grated	50g
Salt and pepper	
Butter, melted	25g
Milk	75ml

Method

Peel and finely slice the potatoes. Butter the Remoska and cover the base with half the potato slices. Stir together the cream cheese, defrosted vegetables, the egg, and 2 tablespoons of the grated cheese. Season.

Spread this mixture over the potatoes, cover with remaining potatoes, brush with melted butter, pour over with the milk. Cook until the potatoes are tender, **approx 25-30 minutes.**

Sprinkle the remaining cheese over the potatoes and cook until golden brown, **approx 10-15 minutes.**

Cheese, Leek and Potato Bake

Ingredients	Standard	Grand
Potatoes	500g	1kg
Leeks, large	2	4
Butter	25g	40g
Milk	75ml	150ml
Egg	1	2
Cream, double	2tbsp	4tbsp
Butter	25g	40g
Nutmeg, grated	$\frac{1}{4}$tsp	$\frac{1}{2}$tsp
Salt and pepper		
Cheese, Cheddar, grated	50g	100g

Method

Boil the unpeeled potatoes in lightly salted water until soft. Peel whilst warm and mash them. Clean the leeks, slice finely and gently cook in the butter. Warm the milk to tepid, stir into the mashed potatoes together with the whisked egg, cream, butter, leeks, grated nutmeg and season.

Butter the Remoska and spread the mashed potatoes. Sprinkle with the grated cheese and cook for **approx 20-25 minutes** until golden brown.

Leeks Baked in Cheese

Ingredients	Standard	Grand
Leeks, trimmed, washed and cut in 5cm pieces	500g	1kg
Butter and breadcrumbs to coat the Remoska (keep a few breadcrumbs for sprinkling on top)		
Eggs	2	4
Cream, double	100ml	200ml
Cheese, Cheddar or Tasty Lancashire	150g	300g
Nutmeg, ground to taste		
Salt and black pepper to taste		

Method

Boil the leeks in lightly salted water until just tender. Drain well and place in the buttered and breadcrumb coated Remoska. Whisk together the cream, cheese and nutmeg and pour over the leeks. Sprinkle with breadcrumbs.

Bake for **approx 15-20 minutes.**

Desserts

Apple and Almond Cream Pie

Ingredients	Standard	Grand
Pastry, short crust	375g	550g
Marzipan, crumbled	150g	225g
Butter	75g	110g
Flour, plain	1½tbsp	2tbsp
Eggs, beaten	1½	2
Apples, cooking, peeled, sliced	2	3
Lemon juice	1tbsp	1½tbsp
Sugar	2tbsp	3tbsp
Milk for glazing		

Method

Roll out half the pastry to fit the base of the Remoska and put into the Remoska. Put the marzipan and butter into a food processor and blend until smooth. Add the flour and eggs and blend until creamy. Spread over the pastry base.

Toss the apple slices with the lemon juice and sugar. Place on the almond cream, mounding them in the centre.

Roll out the remaining pastry and brush the edges with milk. Invert onto the apples, sealing the edges well. Brush with milk and cut a few slits in the top.

Cook in the Remoska for **approx 40-50 minutes** until golden and the pastry is cooked through. Serve warm or cold.

Apple and Walnut Bread Pudding

Ingredients	Standard	Grand
Eggs	3	5
Condensed milk, can	397g	1½ cans
Water, hot	200ml	300ml
Vanilla extract	1tsp	1½tsp
Cinnamon, ground	1tsp	1½tsp
Butter, melted	55g	75g
Bread, white, cubed	175g	265g
Apples, cooking, peeled, chopped	3	5
Walnuts, chopped	75g	120g

Method

Whisk together the eggs, condensed milk, water, vanilla, cinnamon and butter until blended. Stir in the bread cubes until completely moistened. Stir in the apples and walnuts.

Put into the Remoska and cook for **approx 45-50 minutes** until browned and cooked through. Serve warm with whipped cream.

Apple Pudding

Ingredients	Standard	Grand
Flour, self-raising	225g	350g
Salt, pinch		
Cloves, pinch		
Cinnamon, ground	1tsp	2tsp
Butter	110g	175g
Lemon zest	1	2
Lemon juice	1tbsp	2tbsp
Sugar, caster	110g	175g
Apples, cooking, peeled, chopped	3	5
Eggs, beaten	2	3
Milk to mix		
Sugar, caster to sprinkle		

Method

Sift the flour, salt and spices into a mixing bowl. Rub in the butter until the mixture resembles breadcrumbs. Stir in the lemon zest, lemon juice, sugar and apples until combined. Add the eggs and enough milk to make a soft dough.

Line the base of the Remoska with a circle of *Magic Non-Stick Liner*. Put the dough into the Remoska and sprinkle with 1-2 tablespoons sugar.

Cook for **approx 30-40 minutes**, until golden brown. Cool in the Remoska for **15 minutes** before serving.

Baked Pears in Greek Honey and Wine

Ingredients	Standard	Grand
Pears	3	5-6
Lemon juice	3tsp	5-6tsp
Cinnamon stick, broken	1	2
Greek honey	125ml	190ml
Wine, Greek, red dessert	125ml	190ml
Lemon peel strips	2	3-4

Method

Peel, core and halve the pears and put into the Remoska. Sprinkle with lemon juice. Add the cinnamon stick. Drizzle over the honey and pour in the wine. Add the lemon peel. Cook in the Remoska for **20 minutes.**

Turn the pears over and cook for a **further 15-20 minutes** until the pears are tender. Put the pears into a serving dish and pour over the honey and wine, discarding the lemon peel.

The honey and wine should be syrupy. If not, continue cooking for a few minutes in the Remoska.

Serve warm or cold with crème fraiche.

Baked Pears with Pecan Stuffing

Ingredients	Standard	Grand
Pears	4	6
Lemon juice	2tbsp	3tbsp
Nuts, pecan, coarsely chopped	5tbsp	7tbsp
Sultanas	4tbsp	6tbsp
Honey	2tbsp	3tbsp
Sugar, light brown	2tsp	3tsp
Cinnamon	1tsp	3tsp
Butter, melted	1tbsp	1½tbsp
Pear juice	150ml	225ml

Method

Peel, halve and core the pears, removing enough core to make a nice hollow inside the pear. Brush the pears with the lemon juice and place in the Remoska. Mix together the pecans, sultanas, honey, sugar, cinnamon and butter to form a paste. Spoon mixture into the pear hollows.

Pour the pear juice around the pears. Cook for **approx 30-40 minutes,** (depending on the ripeness of the pears) until the pears are tender, basting the pears with the juices once or twice during cooking.

Serve warm with whipped cream or ice cream.

Berry Friands

Ingredients	Standard or Grand
Egg whites	3
Butter, melted	90g
Almonds, ground	60g
Sugar, icing	120g
Flour, plain	50g
Raspberries	50g
Strawberries, sliced	50g
Icing sugar for dusting	

Method

Whisk the egg whites lightly with a fork. Stir in the remaining ingredients, except the strawberries, until just combined.

Spoon into silicone cake cases and top with strawberry slices.

Put into the Remoska (6 at a time in the Standard and 12 in the Grand). Cook for **approx 20-25 minutes** until golden brown. Sift over a little icing sugar just before serving.

Chocolate and Amaretto Puddings

Ingredients	Standard	Grand
Amaretti biscuits	8	12
Amaretto liqueur	2tbsp	3tbsp
Butter	100g	150g
Chocolate, plain 70%	100g	150g
Eggs	2	3
Sugar, caster	100g	150g
Almonds, ground	70g	105g
Flour, plain	1tbsp	$1\frac{1}{2}$tbsp
Baking powder	$\frac{1}{2}$tsp	$\frac{3}{4}$tsp

Method

Butter 4 individual pudding basins (6 for the Grand) and place an amaretto biscuit in each basin. Moisten the biscuits with a little liqueur. Melt the butter and chocolate in a heatproof bowl over a pan of simmering (not boiling) water or in a microwave oven. Set aside to cool slightly.

Whisk the eggs and sugar until pale, thick and mousse-like. Whisk in the melted chocolate. Gently stir in the ground almonds, flour and baking powder until well blended.

Spoon into the basins to half fill them. Place an amaretto biscuit in each, then top with the remaining mixture. Cover the tops with greased foil.

Put into the Remoska. Pour in hot water to come halfway up the basins. Cook for **approx 25-30 minutes,** until firm to the touch, but still moist inside. Serve warm with pouring cream.

amaretti biscuits

Coconut Milk and Honey Puddings

Ingredients	Standard	Grand
Honey	6tsp	12tsp
Butter	85g	170g
Sugar, caster	110g	220g
Eggs, beaten	2	4
Flour, self-raising	120g	240g
Salt, pinch		
Coconut milk	4tbsp	8tbsp
Vanilla extract, few drops		

Method

Lightly butter 2 individual pudding bowls (4 for the Grand) and put 3 teaspoons of honey into the base of each. Beat the butter until soft, then beat in the sugar until creamy and smooth. Gradually beat in the eggs until blended. Sift in the flour and salt and stir until blended. Stir in the coconut milk and vanilla.

Spoon into the pudding bowls and put into the Remoska. Pour in hot water to come halfway up the bowls.

Cook in the Remoska for **approx 30-40 minutes** until risen and golden.

Turn out onto plates and serve with whipped cream.

Cranberry, Orange and Walnut Pudding

Ingredients	Standard	Grand
Cranberries, dried	220g	330g
Orange juice	4tbsp	6tbsp
Milk	50ml	75ml
Breadcrumbs, fresh	200g	300g
Sugar, caster	110g	175g
Egg	1	2 medium
Orange zest	1	1
Walnuts, roughly chopped	75g	125g

Method

Soak the cranberries in the orange juice for at least 2 hours. Heat the milk in a pan and bring to the boil. Remove from the heat and add the breadcrumbs. Stir well and leave until almost cold. Beat the breadcrumb mixture until thick and then beat in the egg, most of the sugar, orange zest and walnuts. Stir in the soaked cranberries.

Put into the Remoska and sprinkle with the remaining sugar. Bake for **approx 30-40 minutes** until golden.

Serve hot or cold with custard or whipped cream.

Honey Baked Apples with Blackberries

Ingredients	Standard	Grand
Apples, Bramley	4	6
Honey	4tbsp	6tbsp
Cinnamon	1tsp	1½tsp
Orange, zest and juice	1	2
Blackberries	250g	375g

Method

Core the apples, cut round the skin of the apples with a sharp knife and place in the Remoska. Mix together the honey, cinnamon and orange zest and place an equal amount in the cavity of each apple. Pour the orange juice around the apples.

Cook for **20 minutes,** basting with the orange juice occasionally.

Spoon the blackberries over and around the apples and cook for a **further 10-15 minutes,** until the apples are tender.

Spoon the juices and blackberries over the apples to serve.

Little Lime Puddings

Ingredients	Standard	Grand
Limes	4	6
Butter	50g	75g
Sugar, caster	125g	185g
Eggs, separated	2	3
Flour, self-raising	55g	75g
Milk	150ml	225ml
Cream, double	150ml	225ml

Method

Finely grate the zest of 1 lime (2 for the Grand) into a mixing bowl. Squeeze the juice from all the limes and set aside. Beat together the butter, sugar and lime zest until pale and fluffy. Beat in the egg yolks, then the flour until combined. Stir in the milk, cream and lime juice - the mixture will curdle.

Whisk the egg whites until they stand in soft peaks, then fold into the lime mixture until blended.

Divide between 4 (6-8 for the Grand) greased individual pudding basins and stand in the Remoska. Pour in boiling water to come halfway up the sides of the basins. Cook for **approx 35-40 minutes** until the tops are light golden. The puddings will have separated into a lime custard layer under a light sponge.

Serve immediately.

lime

Luxury Chocolate Pots

Ingredients	Standard	Grand
Egg yolks	2	4
Sugar, caster	$\frac{1}{2}$tbsp	1tbsp
Vanilla extract	$\frac{1}{2}$tsp	1tsp
Cream, double	225ml	450ml
Chocolate, plain 70%	100g	200g

Method

Whisk the egg yolks, sugar and vanilla together lightly. Put the cream and chocolate in a pan and heat gently until the chocolate has melted. Remove from the heat and stir gently. Pour the warm mixture into the egg yolks, whisking constantly until blended. Pour into 2-3 ramekins or ovenproof dishes, for the Standard and 4-5 ramekins for the Grand.

Place the dishes in the Remoska and pour in enough boiling water to come 1cm up the sides of the dishes. Cook for **approx 15-20 minutes,** until a skin has formed on the surface.

Cool and chill for at least **1 hour** before serving.

Magic Coconut Pie

Ingredients	Standard	Grand
Eggs	4	6
Butter, melted	50g	75g
Sugar, caster	110g	175g
Flour, self-raising	75g	150g
Salt, pinch		
Milk	425ml	635ml
Desiccated coconut	110g	175g
Vanilla extract	1tsp	1½tsp

Method

Whisk all the ingredients together until thoroughly combined. Pour into the Remoska and cook for **approx 30 minutes** for the Standard and **approx 45-50 minutes** for the Grand until the top is firm.

As this cooks it forms a crust on the bottom, a custard filling and coconut topping. Serve it warm straight from the Remoska.

Malva Pudding (South African)

Ingredients	Standard	Grand
Sugar, caster	180g	270g
Eggs	2	3
Jam, apricot	1tbsp	2tbsp
Butter, melted	1tbsp	1½tbsp
Vinegar, white wine	1tsp	1½tsp
Flour, plain	150g	225g
Bicarbonate of soda	1tsp	1½tsp
Salt	¼tsp	½tsp
Milk	90ml	180ml
For the sauce:		
Cream, whipping	200ml	300ml
Butter, melted	100g	150g
Sugar, caster	120g	180g
Hot water	90ml	130ml
Vanilla extract	1tsp	1½tsp

Method

Beat together the sugar, eggs, and jam with an electric whisk until thick and light. Add the butter, followed by the vinegar and mix well. Stir in the flour, bicarbonate of soda and salt with the milk. Beat well.

Line the base of the Remoska pan with a circle of *Magic Non-Stick Liner*. Pour the mixture into the Remoska and cook for **approx 25-30 minutes** until well browned and risen.

Switch off the Remoska, but leave the pudding in the Remoska.

For the sauce: heat all the ingredients together in a pan over a low heat until the sugar has dissolved. Bring to the boil and pour over the hot pudding in the Remoska.

Maple and Pecan Self-saucing Pudding

Ingredients	Standard	Grand
Flour, plain	125g	185g
Baking powder	3tsp	4½tsp
Salt, pinch		
Maple syrup	90ml	135ml
Milk	150ml	225ml
Egg, beaten	1 med	1 large
Butter, unsalted, melted	65g	125g
Pecan nuts, chopped	75g	100g
For the topping:		
Sugar, light brown	140g	210g
Maple syrup	4tbsp	6tbsp
Water	200ml	300ml

Method

Put all the pudding ingredients, except the pecans into a bowl and whisk well until smooth and blended. Stir in the pecans. Place into the Remoska.

For the topping: put all the topping ingredients into a pan and heat gently until the sugar has dissolved. Bring to the boil and pour over the pudding mixture.

Cook for **approx 30 minutes** until the pudding is cooked and firm to the touch and the sauce is bubbling. Switch off the Remoska and leave the pudding to cool for **approx 10-15 minutes**. Turn out into a serving dish (with the sauce on top) and serve warm with ice cream.

pecan nuts

Marmalade Bread and Butter Pudding

Ingredients	Standard	Grand
Bread, white, thick slices	8	12
Butter	50g	75g
Orange marmalade	$\frac{1}{2}$ jar	$\frac{3}{4}$ jar
Eggs	3	4
Egg yolks	3	4
Sugar, caster	75g	110g
Cream, single	300ml	450ml
Milk	300ml	450ml

Method

Spread the bread with the butter and then the marmalade. Cut into quarters and place in the Remoska. Whisk together the eggs, egg yolks, sugar, cream and milk and pour over the bread to cover completely.

Cook in the Remoska for **approx 35-45 minutes** until golden. Serve warm or cold with cream.

eggs

Orange Dumplings in Caramel Sauce

Ingredients	Standard	Grand
Flour, plain	225g	350g
Baking powder	2tsp	3tsp
Butter	150g	225g
Sugar, light muscovado	55g	75g
Orange, zest and juice	1	2
For the sauce:		
Butter	40g	60g
Sugar, dark muscovado	300g	450g
Water	600ml	900ml

Method

Sift the flour and baking powder into a mixing bowl and rub in the butter until the mixture resembles breadcrumbs. Alternatively do this in a food processor. Stir in the sugar and orange zest and just enough orange juice to mix to a soft dough.

With floured hands roll the dough into balls (7 for the Standard and 10-11 for the Grand).

For the sauce: Put the butter, sugar and water in a pan and bring to the boil, stirring.

Put the dough balls into the Remoska and pour over the sauce. Cook in the Remoska for **approx 25-30 minutes** until the dumplings are cooked. Serve with whipped cream.

Pineapple and Coconut Puddings

Ingredients	Standard	Grand
Pineapple, crushed	227g	300g
Butter	90g	135g
Sugar, caster	125g	185g
Eggs	2	3
Flour, self-raising	60g	120g
Desiccated coconut	2tbsp	3tbsp
Coconut milk	2tbsp	3tbsp

Method

Butter 4 (6 for the Grand) individual 150ml pudding basins and spoon the drained crushed pineapple onto the base of each basin. Beat the butter and sugar until light and creamy. Gradually beat in the eggs. Gently fold in the flour, coconut and coconut milk. Divide the mixture between the basins.

Put into the Remoska (4 in the Standard; 6 in the Grand) and cook for **approx 25-30 minutes** until firm to the touch. Turn out and serve with whipped cream or ice cream.

Pineapple Toffee Pudding

Ingredients	Standard	Grand
Flour, self-raising	125g	185g
Sugar	110g	165g
Pineapple, pieces, drained	200g	300g
Milk	250ml	375ml
Butter, melted	75g	112g
Egg, beaten	1	2
Sugar, light muscovado	130g	190g
Golden syrup	3tbsp	5tbsp
Water	250ml	375ml

Method

Put the flour and sugar into a mixing bowl. Add the pineapple, milk, butter and egg and mix well until blended. Put into the Remoska.

Put the sugar, syrup and water in a pan and heat gently until the sugar has dissolved completely. Bring to the boil, and then pour over the mixture in the Remoska.

Cook for **approx 35-40 minutes** until risen and golden. Serve warm from the Remoska, or turn out upside down onto a serving plate. Serve with cream or custard.

Plum, Walnut and Cinnamon Crumble

Ingredients	Standard	Grand
Butter	125g	185g
Sugar, light muscovado	175g	250g
Plums, halved, stoned	450g	675g
Cinnamon	2tsp	3tsp
Flour, plain	175g	250g
Walnuts, finely chopped	55g	75g

Method

Melt half the butter and half the sugar in a pan over a low heat, stirring. Add the plums and cinnamon, cover and cook gently for **5 minutes**. Put the flour into a bowl and rub in the remaining butter. Stir in the remaining sugar and the walnuts.

Tip the plum mixture into the Remoska and sprinkle the crumble evenly over the top, to completely cover the plums.

Cook for **approx 10-15 minutes** until the crumble is golden. Serve hot with custard or cream.

Rhubarb Crumble Cake

Ingredients	Standard	Grand
Rhubarb, young pink, 1cm pieces	450g	675g
Sugar, caster	1tbsp	1½tbsp
Ginger, ground	1tsp	1½tsp
Butter	110g	175g
Sugar, caster	110g	175g
Eggs, beaten	2	3
Flour, self-raising	110g	175g
Milk		
For the crumble:		
Flour, plain	110g	175g
Sugar, caster	4tbsp	6tbsp
Butter	90g	135g

Method

Toss the rhubarb with the sugar and ginger until coated. Beat the butter and caster sugar until light and creamy. Gradually beat in the eggs until smooth. Sift in the flour and stir until blended. Add a little milk if the mixture is too stiff to drop from a spoon.

Spread the cake mixture over the base of the Remoska. Pile the rhubarb on top.

For the crumble: stir the flour and sugar together and rub in the butter roughly, until crumbly.

Scatter the crumble over the rhubarb and cook for **approx 40-45 minutes** until the crumble is golden and the cake and rhubarb are cooked. Switch off the Remoska and leave to cool for **15 minutes** before removing. Serve warm or cold.

ginger

St. Clements Pudding

Ingredients	Standard	Grand
Butter	90g	135g
Sugar, caster	300g	450g
Eggs	3	4 large
Orange, finely grated, zest and juice	1	1 large
Lemon, finely grated, zest and juice	1	2 small
Flour, plain	75g	140g
Baking powder	1tsp	1½tsp

Method

Beat the butter and sugar until light and creamy. Beat in the eggs until smooth. Gradually beat in the orange and lemon zests and juices, until blended. Stir in the flour and baking powder until well mixed.

Pour into the Remoska and cook for **approx 45-50 minutes** until the top is set and golden, with the sauce underneath. Serve from the Remoska.

Sticky Banoffee Pudding

Ingredients	Standard	Grand
Butter	175g	250g
Sugar, dark brown	150g	225g
Flour, self-raising	175g	250g
Eggs, beaten	3	4
Bananas, sliced	3	4
Lemon, juice	1	2
Chocolate, plain, chopped	100g	150g
Pecan nuts	100g	150g
Carnation Caramel	200g	300g

Method

Beat the butter and sugar until soft and light. Beat in the flour and eggs until smooth.

Gently stir in the bananas, lemon juice, chocolate, pecans and two thirds of the caramel. Put into the Remoska and dot the remaining caramel on top. Cook for **approx 35-45 minutes** until browned and bubbling.

Sticky Toffee Pudding

Ingredients	Standard	Grand
Water	575ml	900ml
Dates, dried	200g	400g
Baking powder	1tsp	2tsp
Butter	100g	200g
Sugar, caster	150g	300g
Eggs, beaten	3	5
Flour, self-raising	125g	200g
Mixed spice	1tsp	$1\frac{1}{2}$tsp
For the sauce:		
Sugar, light muscovado	100g	200g
Butter	100g	200g
Golden syrup	100g	200g
Cream, double	300ml	575ml
Vanilla essence	3 drops	4 drops

Method

Chop the dates and pour boiling water over. Leave to cool. Beat together the butter and sugar until light and fluffy. Gradually beat in the eggs. Fold in the sieved flour, baking powder and mixed spice.

Stir in the soaked dates and pour into the Remoska. Cook for **approx 35-40 minutes** until browned and firm to the touch.

For the sauce: put all the ingredients in a pan over a low heat and stir until the sugar has dissolved.

Add the cream. Simmer, stirring, until golden brown.

Cut the pudding into wedges and serve with the warm sauce.

Stuffed Nectarines in White Wine

Ingredients	Standard	Grand
Nectarines, halved and stones removed	4-6	6-9
Amaretti biscuits, crushed to crumbs	100g	150g
Butter	100g	150g
Sugar, caster	85g	130g
Egg, beaten	1 medium	1 large
Almonds, ground	85g	130g
Wine, white	100ml	150ml

Method

Mix together the amaretti crumbs, butter, sugar, egg and ground almonds until blended. Push the mixture into the cavities of the nectarines, piling it on top and pressing down lightly. Put into the Remoska and pour the white wine around the nectarines.

Cook for **approx 30 minutes** until golden and crisp and the fruit is soft.

Serve warm with the juices and whipped cream or ice cream.

nectarines

White Chocolate and Raspberry Pudding

Ingredients	Standard	Grand
Flour, plain	125g	190g
Baking powder	2tsp	3tsp
Sugar	60g	90g
Chocolate, white, chopped	80g	120g
Vanilla extract	1tsp	1½tsp
Milk	60ml	90ml
Egg, beaten	1 medium	1 large
Butter, melted	60g	90g
Raspberries, frozen	130g	195g
For the sauce:		
Sugar, caster	110g	175g
Cornflour	2tsp	3tsp
Milk	310ml	465ml
Chocolate, white, chopped	100g	150g

Method

Sift the flour and baking powder into a mixing bowl. Add the sugar and chocolate. Whisk together the vanilla, milk, egg and butter until blended. Gently stir into the flour mixture. Fold in the raspberries. Spoon into the Remoska and smooth the surface.

For the sauce: mix together the sugar and cornflour and whisk with a little of the milk. Put the remaining milk and chocolate in a pan and stir over a low heat until the chocolate has melted. Whisk in the sugar and cornflour and pour over the pudding mixture.

Cook in the Remoska for **approx 40-50 minutes** until the pudding is golden and cooked through.

Serve immediately.

Baking

Almond Pies

Ingredients	Standard and Grand
Butter	110g
Sugar, icing	110g
Almonds, ground	110g
Flour, plain	30g
Eggs	3
Almond extract	1tsp
Almonds, flaked	50g
Pastry, puff	
(pack of 6 ready-made rounds)	
Sugar, caster to sprinkle	

Method

Whisk together the butter, icing sugar, ground almonds, flour, 2 eggs and almond extract until smooth. Stir in the flaked almonds. Spread the mixture over 3 rounds of pastry, leaving a 1cm border. Beat the remaining egg and brush the borders.

Place the remaining 3 pastry rounds on top and press to seal. Cut a slit in the top of each. Brush with the remaining beaten egg and sprinkle lightly with caster sugar. Place 1 pie in the Standard Remoska (2 in the Grand; they will be touching but will still cook evenly).

Cook for **25 minutes** until the pastry is golden.

Cool on a wire rack.

almonds

Apple, Walnut and Cinnamon Cake

Ingredients	Standard	Grand
Eggs	2	3
Vanilla extract	1tsp	2tsp
Sugar	125g	250g
Butter, melted	50g	110g
Apples, peeled and sliced	2	4
Orange, grated zest	$\frac{1}{2}$	1
Flour, plain	110g	200g
Baking powder	1tsp	2tsp
Milk	50ml	100ml
Sultanas	60g	120g
Walnuts, chopped	50g	100g
Sugar, Demerara	$1\frac{1}{2}$tbsp	3tbsp
Cinnamon	2tsp	4tsp

Method

Whisk together the eggs, vanilla and sugar until thick and creamy. Whisk in the butter, flour, baking powder and milk until well blended. Put half the mixture into a 17cm shallow cake tin for the Standard or 24cm cake tin for the Grand, top with half the apples, orange zest, sultanas and walnuts.

Repeat with the remaining mixture finishing with the layer of apples, orange zest and sultanas. Mix the sugar with the cinnamon and sprinkle over the fruit. Place the cake tin in the Remoska and bake for **approx 35-40 minutes** in the Standard and **approx 1 hour** in the Grand. Switch off and leave the tin in the Remoska for **20 minutes**, then lift out the cake tin and turn the cake onto a wire rack to cool.

Serve warm with whipped cream or ice cream.

apple

Apricot & Cherry Rock Buns

Ingredients	Standard and Grand
Butter	75g
Sugar, caster	75g
Almonds, ground	75g
Apricots, dried, no need to soak	50g
Glacé cherries	50g
Flour, plain	140g
Eggs, beaten	2
Rosewater, optional	1tsp
Beaten egg to glaze	

Method

Line the base of the Remoska with a circle of *Magic Non-Stick Liner*. Cream the butter and sugar until light and creamy. Add the ground almonds, apricots and cherries, then sift in the flour, add the eggs and rosewater. Mix to a stiff dough.

Place small mounds of the mixture in the Remoska. Brush the buns with a little beaten egg and bake for **approx 12-15 minutes** until golden. Cool on a wire rack.

apricots

Banana and Pecan Monkey Bread

Ingredients	Grand
Yeast, easy-blend	7g sachet
Flour, strong, plain	500g
Salt	$\frac{1}{2}$ tsp
Sugar, caster	1tbsp
Bananas, very ripe	2
Lemon juice	1tbsp
Lemon zest, finely grated	2tsp
Egg, beaten	1
Milk, warm	200ml
For the coating:	
Pecans, finely chopped	110g
Ground cinnamon	2tsp
Sugar, light muscovado	110g
Butter, melted	75g

Method

Mix together the yeast, flour, salt and sugar in a mixing bowl and make a well in the centre. Mash the bananas with the lemon juice and zest. Add the egg and enough warm milk to the yeast mixture to form a soft dough. Knead in the mashed bananas. Knead on a lightly floured surface until smooth and elastic. Put into a greased bowl, cover with cling film and leave in a warm place to rise for **approx 40-60 minutes** until doubled in size.

Mix together the pecans, cinnamon and sugar in a small bowl.

Knead the dough lightly on a floured surface and divide into 20-25 balls. Dip the balls into the melted butter and roll in the pecan mixture. Arrange the balls in the Remoska, spaced slightly apart and top with the remaining dough balls. Sprinkle with any remaining pecan mixture and melted butter. Cover with cling film and leave in a warm place for **approx 40-45 minutes** until risen and puffy.

Remove the cling film. Switch on the Remoska and cook for **approx 25-35 minutes** until risen and golden.

Banana and Walnut Cupcakes

Ingredients	Standard
Bananas	2
Eggs	3
Butter	150g
Sugar	150g
Flour, plain	150g
Baking powder	1tsp
Walnuts	50g
For the topping:	
Banana, ripe	1
Cream, double	100ml
Sugar, icing	2tbsp
Cream cheese	2tbsp
Lemon juice	1tbsp

Method

Mash the bananas. Beat the eggs with the butter and sugar until well blended. Beat in the banana, then stir in the walnuts. Sift in the flour and baking powder and lightly mix in, until just combined. Spoon the mixture into 12 silicone cupcake cases and place 6 cases in the Remoska. Cook for **approx 15-20 minutes** until golden and springy to the touch.

Remove and place on a wire rack to cool. Repeat with the remaining cupcake cases. Unmould the cakes.

For the topping: mash the banana and beat in the cream, icing sugar, cream cheese and lemon juice until thick and smooth.

Spread the topping on the cakes.

walnuts

Black Forest Cupcakes

Ingredients	Standard and Grand
Butter	150g
Sugar	110g
Vanilla extract	1tsp
Eggs, beaten	2
Flour, plain	200g
Cocoa powder	25g
Baking powder	2tsp
Milk	6-8tbsp
Plain chocolate, 60% cocoa solids, grated	50g
For the topping:	
Cream, double	200ml
Cherry compote or jam	10-12tbsp
Plain chocolate, 60% cocoa solids, grated	50g

Method

Beat the butter with an electric whisk until soft. Gradually beat in the sugar and vanilla until very creamy. Gradually beat in the eggs until blended. Sift in the flour, cocoa and baking powder alternately with the milk and fold in gently until combined. Stir in the grated chocolate.

Spoon the mixture into 12 silicone cupcake cases. Place the cases in the Remoska (6 at a time for the Standard and 12 in the Grand). Cook for **approx 20-25 minutes** until springy to the touch. Remove and place on a wire rack to cool and unmould.

For the topping: whisk the cream until thick and spoon into a piping bag. Pipe the cream onto the top of each cake. Decorate as you wish with cherry jam, grated chocolate or a whole cherry. Serve chilled.

Breakfast Bake

Ingredients	Standard	Grand
Eggs	3	6
Milk	225ml	450ml
Pepper, freshly ground		
Mustard, grainy	$\frac{1}{2}$tsp	1tsp
Bread, thick slices, cubed	3	6
Oil	1tbsp	2tbsp
Sausages	4	6
Cheese, Cheddar, grated (optional)	55g	110g

Method

Beat together the eggs, milk, salt, pepper and mustard. Stir in the bread cubes and leave to stand in the fridge for **4-5 hours**. Heat the oil in a frying pan and brown the sausages on all sides. Remove from pan and cut into slices.

Put the egg mixture into the Remoska. Place the sausages on top and sprinkle the cheese, if using.

Cook for **approx 20 minutes** until golden, risen and cooked through. Stand for **10 minutes** before serving.

Cereal Macaroons

Ingredients	Standard	Grand
Egg, white	1	2
Salt, pinch		
Sugar, caster	$\frac{1}{2}$ cup	1 cup
Desiccated coconut	$\frac{1}{2}$ cup	1 cup
Rice Krispies	$\frac{1}{2}$ cup	1 cup
Vanilla extract	$\frac{1}{2}$tsp	1tsp

Use a 225g measuring cup to measure the ingredients.

Method

Whisk the egg whites and salt until softly peaking. Whisk in the sugar a little at a time until stiff. Gradually fold in the rest of the ingredients.

Line the base of the Remoska with a circle of *Magic Non-Stick Liner.*

Drop in small heaps on the non-stick liner. Bake for **approx 10 minutes** until light golden. Switch off the Remoska, but leave the lid on and leave until the macaroons are cold and firm.

Cheese and Ham Scones

Ingredients	Grand
Flour, self-raising	225g
Baking powder	2tsp
Salt, pinch	
Butter	25g
Cheese, strong Cheddar, grated	55g
Ham, cooked, chopped	55g
Milk	150ml
Egg to glaze	

Method

Line the base of the Remoska pan with a circle of *Magic Non-Stick Liner*. Sift the flour, baking powder and salt into a mixing bowl. Rub in the butter, and then stir in the grated cheese and chopped ham.

Make a well in the centre of the mixture and pour in just enough milk to form soft but not sticky dough. Turn out onto a floured surface and knead lightly until smooth. Roll or pat out to a thickness of 2cm. Cut into 12 rounds with a 6cm cutter. Brush the tops lightly with a little beaten egg.

Place 6 scones in the Remoska and bake for **approx 15-20 minutes** until golden brown. Cool on a wire rack. Repeat with the remaining scones.

These are delicious split and spread with butter or cream cheese.

Chocolate Cake

Ingredients	Standard
Butter	225g
Sugar, caster	225g
Eggs	4
Flour, self raising	225g
Cocoa powder	50g
For the topping:	
Chocolate, plain	150g
Cream, double	50ml

Method

Cream the butter, sugar and add the eggs one at a time with a little flour to prevent curdling. Fold in the rest of the sifted flour with the cocoa powder. Spoon into the lightly greased Remoska and bake for **approx 40 minutes.**

For the topping: when the cake is cold, melt the chocolate, stir in the cream and spread on top of the cake.

Chocolate Cherry Cake

Ingredients	Grand
For the base:	
Plain chocolate digestive biscuits, crushed to crumbs	40g
Butter, melted	110g
For the cake:	
Eggs, large	3
Sugar, caster	150g
Flour, plain	120g
Cornflour	25g
Baking powder	1½tsp
Cocoa powder	4½tbsp
Almond extract	½tsp
Butter, melted	150g
Morello cherries in syrup, drained	680g

Method

For the base: mix together the biscuit crumbs and butter until well blended. Press firmly onto the base of the Remoska and press down with the back of a spoon. Cook in the Remoska for **10 minutes.**

For the cake: whisk the eggs and sugar with an electric whisk until thick and pale. Sift in the flour, cornflour, baking powder and cocoa and stir until combined. Stir in the almond extract and melted butter until blended, gently stir in the cherries.

Spoon on top of the base and continue cooking in the Remoska for **approx 30-35 minutes** until the cake is cooked through. Switch off and leave to cool in the Remoska.

Cut into slices and serve with whipped cream or ice cream.

morello cherries

Coconut Pyramids

Ingredients	Grand
Coconut, desiccated	225g
Condensed milk, half tin	397g
Vanilla Extract	1tsp

Method

Mix the ingredients together until blended. Leave to stand for **5 minutes.**

Line the base of the Remoska with a circle of *Magic Non-Stick Liner.*

Spoon the mixture into egg cups (or other similar size moulds) and unmould 6 into the Remoska. Bake for **approx 15-20 minutes** until golden.

Cool on a wire rack lined with non-stick baking paper. Repeat with the remaining mixture, cooking 6 at a time.

Cupcakes

Ingredients	Grand
Eggs	2
Flour, self-raising	110g
Baking powder	$\frac{1}{2}$tsp
Butter, softened	110g
Sugar	110g
Vanilla Extract	1tsp
For the topping:	
Icing sugar	175g
Hot water	1-2tbsp
Food colouring	

Method

Put all the cupcake ingredients into a mixing bowl and whisk with an electric whisk until well combined. Alternatively beat well with a wooden spoon.

Spoon the mixture into 12 silicone cupcake cases, filling them half full. Place 6 cases in the Remoska. Cook for **15 minutes** until golden and springy to the touch.

Remove and place on a wire rack to cool. Repeat with the remaining cupcake cases. Unmould the cakes.

For the topping: sift the icing sugar into a bowl and gradually stir in the water until smooth and thick. Add a few drops of your choice of food colouring. Spread the icing over the cooled cakes.

Date and Banana Cake

Ingredients	Grand
Dates, dried, pitted, chopped	150g
Orange juice	4tbsp
Butter	125g
Sugar, light muscovado	125g
Orange, unwaxed, finely grated zest	1
Eggs, large	2
Flour, self-raising	175g
Bananas, very ripe, peeled, mashed	150g

Method

Grease a deep 18cm cake tin and line the base with non-stick baking paper. Heat the dates and orange juice in a pan and bring to the boil. Remove from the heat and set aside to cool. Beat the butter, sugar and orange zest in a mixing bowl until smooth and creamy. Beat in the eggs, one at a time adding a little flour with each one. Stir in the remaining flour, dates and banana.

Spoon into the cake tin and level the top. Cook in the Remoska for **approx 40-45 minutes** until risen and golden and cooked through.

Cool in the tin for **10 minutes,** then remove and cool on a wire rack.

Empanadas

Ingredients	Grand
Flour, plain	225g
Turmeric	$\frac{1}{2}$tsp
Chilli flakes	$\frac{1}{2}$tsp
Butter, diced	75g
Salt, pinch	
Milk	50-75ml
Egg yolk	1
Egg, beaten	1
For the filling:	
Olive oil	1tbsp
Onion, finely chopped	1
Garlic clove, crushed	1
Carrot, finely diced	1
Beef, minced	225g
Tomato purée	1tbsp
Cumin ground	$\frac{3}{4}$tsp
Chilli powder	1tsp
Potato, peeled and diced	1
Stout	100ml
Salt and pepper	

stout

Method

Put the flour, turmeric, chilli flakes, butter and salt in a food processor and pulse until the consistency of breadcrumbs. Add the milk and egg yolk and pulse together to form a dough.

Turn the dough out onto a lightly floured surface and knead for a few minutes. Wrap in cling film and chill in the fridge for **1 hour.**

For the filling: heat the oil in a frying pan and fry the onions, garlic and carrot until soft. Add the mince and fry for a few minutes, until browned. Stir in the tomato purée, cumin and chilli powder and cook for **approx 3-4 minutes.**

Add the potatoes and stout and bring to the boil. Reduce the heat and simmer for **approx 20-25 minutes,** until the potatoes are tender. Leave to cool.

Roll out the dough on a floured surface and cut out 10 x 12cm diameter circles.

Place a spoonful of filling in the middle of each pastry circle. Brush the edge of one half of each of the circles with some of the beaten egg, then fold over the other side and press well to seal.

Put into the Remoska and cook for **approx 20-25 minutes,** until the pastry is golden and the filling is hot.

Milk and Honey Buns

Ingredients	Standard	Grand
Flour, strong white	225g	350g
Yeast, fast action	2 sachets	3 sachets
Butter, melted	55g	75g
Egg yolks	2	3
Milk, warmed	75ml	112ml
Honey	2tsp	3tsp
Salt, pinch		
For the topping:		
Milk	120ml	180ml
Honey	2tbsp	3tbsp
Cinnamon		

Method

Mix the flour with the yeast in a mixing bowl. Stir together the butter, egg yolks, milk and honey until smooth. Pour onto the flour and add the salt. Mix well to form soft dough. Knead well until smooth and elastic. Roll pieces of the dough into small balls (6 for the Standard, 10 for the Grand) and place around the edge of the base of the Remoska. Cover with a damp cloth and leave for **approx 50-60 minutes** until doubled in size. Switch on the Remoska and cook for **approx 20 minutes** until golden.

For the topping: heat the milk with half the honey until almost boiling. Remove the Remoska lid, switch off and pour over the milk mixture to soak into the buns. Brush the buns with the remaining honey and sprinkle lightly with cinnamon.

Mini Olive Brioche

Ingredients	Standard and Grand
Butter	25g
Sugar	$\frac{1}{2}$tbsp
Milk	110ml
Egg	1
Flour, strong	275g
Salt	$\frac{1}{2}$tsp
Olives, pitted	12
Yeast, Fast Action	1tsp
For the glaze:	
Egg, beaten	1
Milk	1tsp

Method

Heat the butter, sugar and milk in a pan over a low heat until the sugar has dissolved and the butter has melted. Remove from the heat and leave to cool slightly. Mix the flour, salt and yeast in a mixing bowl. Make a well in the centre and pour in the melted butter mixture and the egg. Mix to a dough and knead for **10 minutes.** Put into a greased bowl, cover with cling film and leave in a warm place for **30 minutes** or until doubled in size.

Knead the dough briefly. Divide into 12 even sized pieces. Place an olive in the palm of your hand and roll a piece of dough into a ball between your palms to enclose the olive. Repeat with the remaining dough. Place the balls in silicone cupcake cases. Cover with cling film and leave to rise for **30 minutes.**

Mix the egg and milk and brush the rolls with the glaze. Put into the Remoska (6 in the Standard; 12 in the Grand) and cook for **approx 20 minutes** until risen and golden. Cool on a wire rack.

olives

Orange and Aniseed Cookies

Ingredients	Standard and Grand
Butter	225g
Sugar, icing	110g
Orange juice	3tbsp
Orange flower water, few drops	
Egg yolk	1
Flour, plain	300g
Orange, grated zest	1
Aniseed	1tsp
Icing sugar to finish	

Method

Cream the butter and sugar until pale and creamy, using an electric whisk. In a separate bowl combine the orange juice, orange flower water and egg yolk; then beat the mixture into the butter, mixing well. In another bowl, combine the flour, orange zest and aniseed and gradually add to the butter mixture beating well to form a soft dough. Wrap the dough in cling film and chill for **1 hour.**

Unwrap the dough and shape into 20-25 balls and place a few at a time, apart, in the Remoska. Bake for **approx 20-25 minutes** until lightly golden. Place on a wire rack to cool completely. Sift over the icing sugar.

Peanut Butter Cupcakes

Ingredients	Standard
Butter	75g
Sugar	150g
Peanut butter	75g
Egg, large	1
Flour, self-raising	110g
Salt	$\frac{1}{4}$tsp
Yoghurt, plain	70ml
Vanilla extract, few drops	

Method

Beat the butter and sugar in a mixing bowl until light. Beat in the peanut butter until smooth, then beat in the egg.

Sift in the flour and salt and gently stir in until blended. Stir in the yoghurt and vanilla.

Spoon into 10-12 silicone cupcake moulds. Put into the Remoska and cook for **approx 20-25 minutes** until risen and golden. You will need to do this in 2 batches in the Standard Remoska. The second batch will cook more quickly than the first, as the Remoska is already hot.

Pesto and Tomato Tarts

Ingredients	Grand
Pastry, puff	500g
Pesto	6tsp
Tomatoes, ripe, sliced	4
Salt and pepper	
Cheese, Parmesan, grated	60g
Milk, for glazing	

Method

Roll out the pastry and cut out 6 x 8cm rounds, about the thickness of a £1 coin. Put 2-3 pastry circles in the Remoska and pinch the edges with your fingers, raising them a little. Prick the bases with a fork.

Spread a little pesto on the base of the pastry rounds and arrange tomato slices on top. Season to taste with salt and pepper and sprinkle grated cheese on top. Brush the edges with a little milk.

Cook in the Remoska for **approx 25-30 minutes** until the cheese has melted and the pastry is golden and cooked through.

Repeat with the remaining pastry rounds and ingredients.

Polenta, Cheese and Pancetta Mini Muffins

Ingredients	Standard and Grand
Pancetta cubes	70g
Flour, plain	75g
Polenta (cornmeal)	75g
Salt	½tsp
Baking powder	1tsp
Cheese, Cheddar, grated	25g
Egg	1
Buttermilk	140ml
Milk	50ml
Butter, melted	40g

Method

Cook the pancetta in a dry frying pan until browned. Drain on kitchen paper.

Mix together the flour, polenta, salt, baking powder and cheese in a large mixing bowl. Stir in the pancetta.

Whisk together the egg, buttermilk and milk, then stir into the dry ingredients with the melted butter.

Spoon into 12 silicone cake cases and put into the Remoska (6 at a time in the Standard and 12 in the Grand). Cook for **approx 25-30 minutes** until golden brown and cooked through.

Serve warm.

cheese

Portuguese Custard Tarts

Ingredients	Standard and Grand
Egg yolks	3
Sugar, caster	110g
Cornflour	2tbsp
Cream, double	230ml
Milk	170ml
Vanilla extract	2tsp
Pastry, puff	300g
Cinnamon	2-3tsp

Method

Put the egg yolks, sugar and cornflour in a pan and whisk together. Gradually whisk in the cream and milk until smooth. Heat, stirring, until the mixture thickens and comes to the boil. Remove from the heat and stir in the vanilla extract. Put the custard into a bowl and cover the surface with cling film (to prevent a skin forming) and leave to cool.

Roll out the pastry thinly. Roll up tightly from the short end and cut the log into 12 x 1cm rounds. Lay each pastry round on a lightly floured surface and roll out each round large enough to line the silicone cases. Press the pastry rounds into the silicone cases. Spoon the cooled custard into the pastry cases and sprinkle with cinnamon. Put into the Remoska (6 at a time in the Standard and 12 in the Grand). Bake for **approx 25-30 minutes**, until the pastry and custard are golden.

Raisin Soda Bread

Ingredients	Standard and Grand
Flour, plain	450g
Bicarbonate of soda	$\frac{3}{4}$tsp
Salt	$\frac{3}{4}$tsp
Cream of tartar	$\frac{3}{4}$tsp
Sugar	$1\frac{1}{2}$tbsp
Buttermilk	335ml
Raisins	60g

Method

Sift the dry ingredients into a mixing bowl.

Make a well in the centre and pour in the buttermilk and add the raisins, mixing quickly with a broad bladed knife, until the mixture forms a soft dough.

Turn out onto a floured surface and knead lightly. Pat or roll out the dough into a round, about 4cm thick and place in the Remoska.

Mark the top into 4 sections and bake for **approx 30-35 minutes**, until golden and risen. Cool on a wire rack covered with a clean tea towel, this keeps the crust soft.

Raspberry Shortcake

Ingredients	Standard	Grand
Flour, plain	225g	350g
Sugar, caster	75g	140g
Butter, diced	150g	200g
Raspberries, frozen	125g	190g
Sugar, icing		

Method

Put the flour, sugar and butter into a food processor and process to a fine powder. Press half the mixture into the base of the Remoska, until it comes together. Scatter over the raspberries, leaving a margin around the edges. Sprinkle over the remaining mixture to cover the raspberries and press together.

Cook for **approx 35-45 minutes** until the top is browned and the shortcake is cooked through.

Cool in the Remoska for **10 minutes**, then turn out carefully and dust with icing sugar.

Rosemary Focaccia

Ingredients	Standard	Grand
Flour, strong white (bread)	180g	350g
Yeast, fast action	$\frac{1}{2}$tsp	1tsp
Salt	$\frac{1}{4}$tsp	$\frac{1}{2}$tsp
Warm water	100m	200ml
Olive Oil	2tbsp	4tbsp
Onion, red chopped	1	2
Rosemary, fresh, chopped	1tbsp	2tbsp
Coarse sea salt		

Method

Mix the flour with the yeast and salt in a mixing bowl. Stir in half the olive oil and mix to a dough. Cover with a tea towel or cling film and leave in a warm place to rise for **approx 45 minutes** until doubled in size. Turn out the dough onto a floured surface and knead well until smooth and elastic. Knead in half the onion and rosemary.

Roll out the dough, to fit the Remoska. Place in the Remoska on a circle of *Magic Non-Stick Liner*. Press into the surface with the knuckles to make small depressions in the dough. Prick the dough several times with a fork. Brush with olive oil and sprinkle with some coarse sea salt and the remaining onion and rosemary. Cover and leave in a warm place to rise for **15 minutes**. Bake for **approx 30-35 minutes** until golden and cooked through. Serve warm.

Sticky Maple Buns

Ingredients	Grand
Milk	175ml
Butter	50g
Eggs, beaten	2
Flour, strong white (bread)	450g
Salt	1tsp
Sugar, caster	50g
Easy-blend yeast	1 x 7g sachet
For the filling:	
Raisins	75g
Maple syrup	3-4tbsp
Ground cinnamon	3tsp
Butter	50g
For the glaze:	
Maple syrup	3tbsp

Method

Heat the milk and butter in a pan until the butter has melted, but don't allow it to become hot. Remove from the heat. Sift the flour into a large mixing bowl and stir in the salt, sugar and yeast. Make a well in the centre and pour in the warm milk mixture and the eggs. Work to a soft dough that leaves the sides of the bowl clean. Turn out on to a floured surface and knead for **approx 7 minutes** until smooth and elastic.

Place the dough in an oiled bowl and cover with cling film. Leave in a warm place for **1-2 hours** until doubled in size. Turn out and knead lightly. Roll out to a rectangle approximately 35 x 28cm.

For the filling: melt the butter and brush over the dough. Drizzle the maple syrup over the dough, leaving a margin around the edges. Sprinkle the raisins and cinnamon on top. Starting at the longer edge, roll up the dough carefully and trim off the ends. Cut into 9 even slices. Cover and leave for **approx 30-40 minutes** until puffy and slightly risen. Place 5 buns in the Standard Remoska or all 9 in the Grand and arrange them next to each other. Sprinkle with 1-2 tablespoons caster sugar and bake for **approx 30 minutes** until well risen and browned.

For the glaze: remove the buns from the Remoska and immediately brush 2-3 times with the maple syrup. Place on a wire rack to cool.

Sun Dried Tomato Rolls

Ingredients	Standard	Grand
Flour, strong bread	375g	560g
Yeast, fast action dried	1 sachet	1½ sachets
Sugar	2tsp	3tsp
Salt	1tsp	1½tsp
Butter, melted	40g	60g
Milk, warm	125ml	185ml
Water, warm	125ml	185ml
Sun-dried tomatoes in oil, drained and chopped	½ jar	¾ jar

Method

Combine the flour, yeast and sugar. Stir in the salt, butter, milk, water (you may not need all the liquid) and tomatoes and mix to a dough. Knead the dough on a floured surface for **10 minutes** until smooth and elastic. Put the dough back into the bowl and cover. Stand in a warm place for **1 hour,** until doubled in size.

Knead the dough for **1 minute** then divide it into 8 equal balls (12 for the Grand). Place the balls in the Remoska, slightly apart. Cover with a damp cloth and leave to rise for **20 minutes.**

Brush the tops with a little milk and bake for **approx 35-40 minutes** until golden brown and cooked through.

Toffee Apple Buns

Ingredients	Standard	Grand
Flour, strong plain	225g	350g
Salt, 1 pinch		
Butter	25g	40g
Yeast, fast-action dried	2tsp	3tsp
Sugar	25g	40g
Milk, warm, extra for brushing	75ml	112ml
For the filling:		
Butter, melted	55g	75g
Sugar, light muscovado	75g	110g
Pecan nuts, chopped	25g	40g
Cinnamon	1tsp	1½tsp
Apples, peeled, cored and chopped	3	5
Honey	4tsp	6tsp

Method

Mix together the flour and salt. Rub in the butter until the mixture resembles breadcrumbs, and then stir in the yeast and sugar. Add the egg and milk and mix well to form a soft dough. Knead the dough for **approx 10 minutes** on a floured surface until smooth.

Roll out the dough on a floured surface to a 30 x 23cm rectangle for the Standard and larger for the Grand. Brush with half the butter.

For the filling: mix the remaining butter with the sugar, nuts, cinnamon and apples. Sprinkle over the dough, leaving a margin around the edge. Roll up from one long end and cut into 9-10 slices for the Standard, (13-15 for the Grand). Place into the Remoska, cover with cling film and leave in a warm place for **approx 1 hour** until doubled in size.

Cook in the Remoska for **approx 25-30 minutes** until golden and cooked through. Brush with a little honey and leave in the Remoska for **5 minutes,** then place on a wire rack to cool.

flour

Toffee Apple Cake

Ingredients	Standard	Grand
Cooking apples, peeled, cored and sliced	450g	670g
Flour, self-raising	225g	350g
Cinnamon	1tsp	2tsp
Butter	85g	140g
Sugar	85g	140g
Eggs, beaten	2	3
Milk	150ml	225ml
For the sauce:		
Butter	55g	75g
Sugar, light muscovado	75g	110g
Water	100ml	150ml

Method

Lightly butter the base of the Remoska and arrange the sliced apples on top. Put the flour, cinnamon, butter and sugar into a food processor and process until the mixture resembles breadcrumbs. Add the eggs and milk and process until smooth. Spoon on top of the apples.

For the sauce: put the butter, sugar and water into a pan and heat, stirring until the sugar has dissolved. Bring to a boil and pour over the cake mixture. Cook in the Remoska for **approx 40 minutes,** until cooked through.

Serve warm with cream or ice cream.

muscavado sugar

Walnut Biscuits

Ingredients	Grand
Walnut oil	6tbsp
Butter	110g
Sugar, light muscovado	150g
Flour, self-raising	250g
Salt	$\frac{1}{4}$tsp
Egg, beaten	1
Walnuts, roughly chopped	75g

Method

Cream together the walnut oil and butter. Stir in the sugar, flour, salt and walnuts. Bind with sufficient egg to form a soft dough. Form the dough into a roll and wrap in cling film. Chill well for at least **4 hours**, or overnight until firm.

Slice the roll into thin rounds with a sharp knife and place in the Remoska. Bake for **approx 20-25 minutes** (depending on thickness) until golden brown.

Cool on a wire rack. The biscuits will crisp as they cool.

Index

VEGETABLES

Baked Polenta with Spinach and Cheese   10
Baked Sweet Potatoes and Apples   11
Braised Little Gem Lettuce   12
Broccoli and Cauliflower Soufflés   13
Broccoli and Cheese Calzone   14
Caponata   15
Chicory with Pears   15
Chorizo and Couscous Stuffed Squash   16
Honey, Lemon & Thyme Roasted Root Vegetables   17
Lamb Stuffed Peppers in Cheese Sauce   18
Leeks Wrapped in Smoked Bacon   19
Peppers Stuffed with Chicken   20
Roast Baby Cabbages   21
Souffléd Tomatoes   22
Spicy Sweet Potato Wedges   23
Stuffed Aubergines   24
Stuffed Pancakes   25
Summer Vegetable Gratin   25
Vegetable Frittata   26
Wine Braised Fennel with Parmesan and Walnuts   27

POTATOES

Classic Pommes Anna   30
Creamy Cheese Potato Bake   31
Fluffy Potato Pancakes   32
Indian Spiced Potatoes   33
Latkes   34
Lemon and Thyme Potatoes   35
Mini Rostis   36
Potato and Fennel Boulangère   37
Potato and Red Wine Galette   37
Potato Daube   38
Potato Gratin with Pancetta   39
Savoury Potato Cake   40
Spiced Sweet Potatoes   41

POULTRY AND GAME

Abruzzi Chicken   44
Chicken and Tomato Bake with Basil   45
Chicken Breasts Stuffed with Basil   46
Chicken Curry   47
Chicken Galantine   48
Chicken with Mushrooms   49
Lemon Thyme Poussin   50
Minted Yoghurt Chicken   50
Pancetta Wrapped Chicken with Leeks   51
Roast Chicken Dinner   52
Roast Pheasant   53
Spanish Style Chicken   53
Spiced Chicken   54
Stuffed Chicken Breasts   54
Stuffed Chicken Breasts with Pancetta   55
Sweet and Sticky Chicken   56
Tandoori Chicken   57
Thai Green Chicken Curry   57
Turkey Olives   58
Venison Casserole   59

MEAT

Beef and Haggis Meat Loaf	62
Beef Potato Pie	63
Beef Steaks in Foil Parcels	64
Egg, Chorizo and Cheese Puffs	65
Ham and Sausage Casserole	66
Hot Beef Loaf	67
Lamb Meatballs with Beans	68
Lamb Shoulder with Peppers	69
Lamb Stuffed Aubergines	70
Lamb with Herb Stuffing	71
Minced Beef Wellington	72
One Pot Lamb Curry with Rice	73
Pigs in Cheese Blankets	74
Sausage and Bacon Bake with Cheese Crust	74
Sausage Puff	75
Sausages with Apple and Red Onion	76
Spiced Roast Pork with Fruit	77
Sticky Sausages	78
Stuffed Lamb Chops with Peppers	79
Teviotdale Pie	79

FISH

Fish Parcels	82
Fish with Olive and Tomato Crust	83
Fishcakes	84
Haddock with Lemon Butter Sauce	85
Halibut Bake	86
Macaroni and Tuna Bake	87
Mediterranean Salmon	88
Oriental Salmon	89
Salmon in Couscous parcels	89
Salmon with Lime and Pancetta	90
Salmon with Peppers and Lemon	90
Trout Baked with Almonds	91

PASTA AND RICE

Baked Pasta Pots	94
Broccoli and Pasta Bake	95
Broken Pasta	96
Chicken and Mushroom Pasta	97
Corn Spoonbread	97
Gnocchi Bake	98
Mince Rice Tomato Bake	99
Mushroom Rice	100
Pasta Timbale	101
Polenta Pizza with Peppers	102
Remoska Risotto	103
Spiced Rice Pilau	104
Turkish Pilaf	105

CHEESE

Camembert Baked in its Box 108
Cheese and Pancetta Pinwheels 109
Cheese and Parsley Gougères 110
Cheese and Thyme Puddings 111
Cheese, Potato and Vegetable Cake 112
Cheese, Leek and Potato Bake 113
Leeks Baked in Cheese 113

DESSERTS

Apple and Almond Cream Pie 116
Apple and Walnut Bread Pudding 117
Apple Pudding 117
Baked Pears in Greek Honey and Wine 118
Baked Pears with Pecan Stuffing 119
Berry Friands 119
Chocolate and Amaretto Puddings 120
Coconut Milk and Honey Puddings 121
Cranberry Orange and Walnut Pudding 121
Honey Baked Apples with Blackberries 122
Little Lime Puddings 123
Luxury Chocolate Pots 124
Magic Coconut Pie 125
Malva Pudding 125
Maple and Pecan Self-saucing Pudding 126
Marmalade Bread and Butter Pudding 127
Orange Dumplings in Caramel Sauce 128
Pineapple and Coconut Puddings 129
Pineapple Toffee Pudding 129
Plum, Walnut and Cinnamon Crumble 130
Rhubarb Crumble Cake 131
St Clements Pudding 132
Sticky Banoffee Pudding 132
Sticky Toffee Pudding 133
Stuffed Nectarines in White Wine 134
White Chocolate and Raspberry Pudding 135

BAKING

Almond Pies 138
Apple, Walnut and Cinnamon Cake 139
Apricot and Cherry Rock Buns 140
Banana and Pecan Monkey Bread 141
Banana and Walnut Cupcakes 142
Black Forest Cupcakes 143
Breakfast Bake 144
Cereal Macaroons 144
Cheese and Ham Scones 145
Chocolate Cake 146
Chocolate Cherry Cake 147
Coconut Pyramids 148
Cupcakes 148
Date and Banana Cake 149
Empanadas 150

BAKING (CONTINUED)

Milk and Honey Buns	151
Mini Olive Brioche	152
Orange and Aniseed Cookies	153
Peanut Butter Cupcakes	153
Pesto and Tomato Tarts	154
Polenta, Cheese and Pancetta Mini-muffins	155
Portuguese Custard Tarts	156
Raisin Soda Bread	156
Raspberry Shortcake	157
Rosemary Focaccia	158
Sticky Maple Buns	159
Sun Dried Tomato Rolls	160
Toffee Apple Buns	161
Toffee Apple Cake	162
Walnut Biscuits	163